OPPOSING
VIEWPOINTS®
SERIES

Government Spending

Other Books of Related Interest:

Opposing Viewpoints Series

Health Care

Labor Unions

Military Draft

Welfare

At Issue Series

What Is the Future of the US Economy?

National Security

Contemporary Issues Companion

Consumerism

Current Controversies Series

Health Care

Homeland Security

The Wage Gap

"Congress shall make no law . . . abridging the freedom of speech, or of the press."

First Amendment to the U.S. Constitution

The basic foundation of our democracy is the First Amendment guarantee of freedom of expression. The Opposing Viewpoints Series is dedicated to the concept of this basic freedom and the idea that it is more important to practice it than to enshrine it.

Government Spending

Mitchell Young, Book Editor

GREENHAVEN PRESS
A part of Gale, Cengage Learning

Detroit • New York • San Francisco • New Haven, Conn • Waterville, Maine • London

Christine Nasso, *Publisher*
Elizabeth Des Chenes, *Managing Editor*

© 2009 Greenhaven Press, a part of Gale, Cengage Learning.

Gale and Greenhaven Press are registered trademarks used herein under license.

For more information, contact:
Greenhaven Press
27500 Drake Rd.
Farmington Hills, MI 48331-3535
Or you can visit our Internet site at gale.cengage.com

For product information and technology assistance, contact us at

Gale Customer Support, 1-800-877-4253
For permission to use material from this text or product, submit all requests online at www.cengage.com/permissions

Further permissions questions can be emailed to permissionrequest@cengage.com

Articles in Greenhaven Press anthologies are often edited for length to meet page require-ments. In addition, original titles of these works are changed to clearly present the main thesis and to explicitly indicate the author's opinion. Every effort is made to ensure that Greenhaven Press accurately reflects the original intent of the authors. Every effort has been made to trace the owners of copyrighted material.

Cover photograph reproduced by permission of Grant Taylor/Stone/Getty Images.

LIBRARY OF CONGRESS CATALOGING-IN-PUBLICATION DATA

Government spending / Mitchell Young, book editor.
   p. cm. -- (Opposing viewpoints)
   Includes bibliographical references and index.
   ISBN-13: 978-0-7377-4004-2 (hardcover)
   ISBN-13: 978-0-7377-4005-9 (pbk.)
   1. Government spending policy--United States--Juvenile literature. 2. United States-- Politics and government--2001---Juvenile literature. 3. United States-- Economic policy--2001---Juvenile literature. I. Young, Mitchell.
   HJ7537.G68 2009
   336.3'90973--dc22
                                                                2008042761

Printed in the United States of America
2 3 4 5 6 7 13 12 11 10 09

Contents

Chapter 1: How Do Politics Affect Government Spending?

Chapter 2: Do Governments Spend Tax Money Wisely?

30.80

Chapter 3: How Do Government Spending Policies Affect the Economy?

Chapter 4: How Must Government Spending Change to Meet Future Challenges?

Why Consider
Opposing Viewpoints?

> *"The only way in which a human being can make some approach to knowing the whole of a subject is by hearing what can be said about it by persons of every variety of opinion and studying all modes in which it can be looked at by every character of mind. No wise man ever acquired his wisdom in any mode but this."*
>
> *John Stuart Mill*

In our media-intensive culture it is not difficult to find differing opinions. Thousands of newspapers and magazines and dozens of radio and television talk shows resound with differing points of view. The difficulty lies in deciding which opinion to agree with and which "experts" seem the most credible. The more inundated we become with differing opinions and claims, the more essential it is to hone critical reading and thinking skills to evaluate these ideas. Opposing Viewpoints books address this problem directly by presenting stimulating debates that can be used to enhance and teach these skills. The varied opinions contained in each book examine many different aspects of a single issue. While examining these conveniently edited opposing views, readers can develop critical thinking skills such as the ability to compare and contrast authors' credibility, facts, argumentation styles, use of persuasive techniques, and other stylistic tools. In short, the Opposing Viewpoints Series is an ideal way to attain the higher-level thinking and reading skills so essential in a culture of diverse and contradictory opinions.

In addition to providing a tool for critical thinking, Opposing Viewpoints books challenge readers to question their own strongly held opinions and assumptions. Most people form their opinions on the basis of upbringing, peer pressure, and personal, cultural, or professional bias. By reading carefully balanced opposing views, readers must directly confront new ideas as well as the opinions of those with whom they disagree. This is not to simplistically argue that everyone who reads opposing views will—or should—change his or her opinion. Instead, the series enhances readers' understanding of their own views by encouraging confrontation with opposing ideas. Careful examination of others' views can lead to the readers' understanding of the logical inconsistencies in their own opinions, perspective on why they hold an opinion, and the consideration of the possibility that their opinion requires further evaluation.

Evaluating Other Opinions

To ensure that this type of examination occurs, Opposing Viewpoints books present all types of opinions. Prominent spokespeople on different sides of each issue as well as well-known professionals from many disciplines challenge the reader. An additional goal of the series is to provide a forum for other, less known, or even unpopular viewpoints. The opinion of an ordinary person who has had to make the decision to cut off life support from a terminally ill relative, for example, may be just as valuable and provide just as much insight as a medical ethicist's professional opinion. The editors have two additional purposes in including these less known views. One, the editors encourage readers to respect others' opinions—even when not enhanced by professional credibility. It is only by reading or listening to and objectively evaluating others' ideas that one can determine whether they are worthy of consideration. Two, the inclusion of such viewpoints encourages the important critical thinking skill of objectively evaluating an author's credentials and bias. This evaluation will illuminate an author's reasons for taking a particular stance on an issue and will aid in readers' evaluation of the author's ideas.

It is our hope that these books will give readers a deeper understanding of the issues debated and an appreciation of the complexity of even seemingly simple issues when good and honest people disagree. This awareness is particularly important in a democratic society such as ours in which people enter into public debate to determine the common good. Those with whom one disagrees should not be regarded as enemies but rather as people whose views deserve careful examination and may shed light on one's own.

Thomas Jefferson once said that "difference of opinion leads to inquiry, and inquiry to truth." Jefferson, a broadly educated man, argued that "if a nation expects to be ignorant and free . . . it expects what never was and never will be." As individuals and as a nation, it is imperative that we consider the opinions of others and examine them with skill and discernment. The Opposing Viewpoints Series is intended to help readers achieve this goal.

David L. Bender and Bruno Leone,
Founders

Introduction

> *"Proponents of every agency think that the agency they are interested in is underfunded. The Park Service could use more money for maintaining parks and facilities. The EPA [Environmental Protection Agency] could use more money to clean up toxic waste sites. The Energy Department could use more money for research into new energy sources like fusion and fuel cells."*
>
> *Eric R. Hedman,*
> *"The Politics and Ethics of*
> *Spending Money on Space Exploration,"*
> *The Space Review, December 19, 2005.*

Between 1975 and 1988 the late U.S. senator William Proxmire issued "Golden Fleece" awards to highlight wasteful, even comical, government spending. The award has since been resurrected by the lobbying group Taxpayers for Common Sense. Items such as a National Science Foundation grant of $84,000 to find out why people fall in love, a quarter of a million dollars to find a "good surfing beach" in Honolulu, or one million dollars to preserve a New Jersey sewer as a museum reinforced the public's idea that governments were careless with taxpayers' money. Yet most people like things the government—or better said, various governments—buy: good schools for children, Social Security's safety net for senior citizens and the disabled, a strong national defense. Few would argue that expenditures on good roads, effective police and fire departments, and well-maintained parks are a waste of resources.

Everyone agrees that governments should try to get the most "bang for the buck"—using public funds in the way that brings the most benefit to the most people. But that all-around success is easier said than achieved; governments must contend with competing interests, all struggling for a share of the pie, and they must make decisions about whether a particular program will actually meet its objectives. Taking a look at spending in one area, the federal government's program for space exploration, will help illustrate the difficulties.

Spending on space exploration is not considered vital to the nation. While some projects, such as military satellites, are necessary for national security, projects devoted to *exploring* space, such as the Apollo missions to the moon or robotic exploration of Mars by the Phoenix Lander, are generally considered luxury items. Many taxpayers see them as wasteful. One technologist involved in space exploration is disappointed in that attitude: "'We shouldn't spend money on space exploration until we've solved our problems here on Earth.' If I had a nickel for every time I've heard or read the previous sentence or variations of it, I would have a very big pile of nickels."

Advocates assert that exploration programs could be more than a luxury—they could be wise investments. The Spanish monarchs Ferdinand and Isabella financed explorer Christopher Columbus, and their investment paid off many times over. Such unforeseen profits are hardly likely to come from space exploration; Columbus knew little about the Western seas into which he was sailing, while we know a great deal about the planets in our neighborhood. Space exploration proponents, however, point to the technological developments that their programs spur and the long-term possibility of exploiting the moon or Mars for resources or even for human habitation. Poverty, disease, and other problems will never be completely solved on Earth, no matter how much money the government throws at them. A relatively small expenditure on space, argue space advocates, could yield big dividends in the future.

Moreover, space exploration proponents believe their projects have value beyond mere economic calculations. The whole nation felt pride when Neil Armstrong planted the American flag on the moon; we all have marveled at the images that unmanned missions to the planets have beamed back to Earth; surely the pure knowledge and beauty we derive from these projects is priceless, say enthusiasts. Yet advocates are in the minority. A 2006 poll by the University of Chicago found that when asked about active government spending in various areas, 14.7% of respondents answered "too little" and 37.4% answered "too much" with regard to space exploration. It finished 21st out of 22 programs in the survey, with only foreign aid receiving less acceptance.

Even if spending on space were overwhelmingly popular, distributing allowances would still be difficult. State and congressional district politics would undoubtedly play a role. A decision might have to be made about whether more funding should go to unmanned exploration, thus sending more federal dollars to Pasadena California's Jet Propulsion Laboratory, or to manned exploration of near-Earth space, benefiting Cape Canaveral in Florida. If manned exploration were given priority, technical questions would arise: should NASA (the National Aeronautical and Space Agency) put money into improving the current space shuttles? Or would investing in a whole new type of spacecraft be a better use of funds?

These types of questions need to be answered for all areas of government spending. Should we use taxpayers' money to achieve a certain goal? If so, what is the most efficient way of using that money? How will the overall economy be affected? Which areas of the country will benefit most? How are these issues decided fairly? These dilemmas must ultimately be solved through the political process.

Opposing Viewpoints: Government Spending examines these issues in further detail. The first chapter explores the politics involved in spending decisions: How Do Politics Affect Spending? Next, the issue of efficiency is addressed: Do Governments Spend Tax Money Wisely? The third chapter investigates the implications of government spending: How Do Government Spending Policies Affect the Economy? A look at the adaptation of government spending concludes the book: How Must Government Spending Change to Meet Future Challenges? The various levels of government face this combination of political, moral, and economic dilemmas when making any decision that involves the use of taxpayers' money. The viewpoints presented here show just how difficult spending issues can be.

OPPOSING
VIEWPOINTS®
SERIES

CHAPTER 1

How Do Politics Affect Government Spending?

Chapter Preface

If you wanted to help out a friend or classmate who needed, for example, a new bicycle tire, you would have to dig into your own pocket. Politicians, however, spend money that ultimately comes from taxpayers. Faced with many potential projects, which could aid the public as a whole or help individuals or communities, politicians sometimes have a hard time turning down requests. These combinations of expenses can lead to overspending, and because politicians are not spending their own money—and at the federal level have almost unlimited power to borrow (or maintain a deficit)—there is little reason for them to turn down spending requests. For politicians who want smaller government, this great freedom to spend taxpayers' money poses a problem. Even those who believe in government's ability to help build a better society sometimes question the extent of government spending. This chapter looks at the political conditions that can help politicians to limit their expenditure of taxpayer dollars.

One longtime question is whether, at least at the federal level, money is spent more frugally when government is divided (the President is of one political party, and the Congress is controlled by another) or united (one party controls both the presidency and the Congress). The evidence seems to show that spending grows less quickly if government is divided. In the late 1990s when the branches were divided, the Republican Congress was reluctant to agree to Democratic President Bill Clinton's spending programs. However, from 2001 until 2007, the Republican Party controlled both Congress and the White House. Despite their traditional support of small government, once in control of these branches of government the Republican leadership increased the growth of expenditures. The lack of restraint on the Republicans' part upset many of their more conservative supporters, who generally favor smaller government and who expected the unified Republican government to result in dramatic cuts.

Of course, not everybody believes in small government. Left-leaning commentators tend to believe government spending can benefit everyone. However, even people who believe in larger government debate the *type* of spending. Some of those people hold that government has basic obligations to the poorer citizens, so the priority for spending must be to meet their needs. Others think that targeted government spending can create economic growth: spending money on roads, education, science, and technology can promote jobs in the private sector. Those people advocate that spending intended for economic growth should be put ahead of aid to the poor.

The articles in this chapter illustrate various sides in related debates—the larger government versus smaller government debate, the debate over which political situation restrains spending, and the debate over the type of spending that is best. Readers will see that these are complex and hotly contested questions.

> "Many conservatives see the current spending outrages as a problem of collusion between moderate Republicans and liberal Democrats."

Spending Policy Divides the Republican Party

Shawn Macomber

The Republican Party is sharply divided over spending issues, writes reporter Shawn Macomber in this viewpoint. After gaining control of Congress in 1994, conservatives expected congressional Republicans to cut spending. Over time, however, moderate Republicans began to work with liberal Democrats. They increased spending and "pork"—money for federal projects aimed at a representative's congressional district. "Supply-sider" Republicans stressed economic growth; they ignored budget deficits and went along with high spending levels. A small group of conservative Republicans did work toward cutting spending. Interviewed for this 2005 article, they offered a prophetic warning of electoral defeat if Congress didn't reform its spending habits. Republicans lost their majority in Congress in the 2006 elections.

As you read, consider the following questions:

1. Do "supply-siders" think the budget deficit is a critical issue? What historical example do they point to in order to justify their belief?

2. What does Congressman Mike Pence believe needs to happen in order to permanently control spending?

3. According to Linda Killian, what has changed for Republican representatives, in terms of spending attitudes, since they gained control of the House in 1994?

"This is a fight for the soul of the Republican Party," Wisconsin Congressman Paul Ryan said. "The moral authority of fiscal conservatism is only valid if we practice what we preach." Ryan looks like a conservative Mr. Smith going to Washington. Outraged by what he sees happening in D.C., Ryan makes little attempt in conversation to mask his distaste for the whole scene. With little prompting, Ryan recounts with a sort of jilted awe how many of his own colleagues pressured him to vote for the $300 billion-plus omnibus spending bill last November [2004]. "This 3,000 page monster lands on my desk about six hours before the vote," Ryan said. "There wasn't time but to leaf through it. And what little bit I actually had a chance to read, I sure didn't like." He voted against it. It passed anyway, 344 to 51.

Economic Dynamism or Fiscal Conservatism?

Traditionally, supply-siders have been reluctant to cede too much ground to "green-eyeshade" Republicanism, which they believe focuses too much on cutting deficits and not enough on clearing the boards to let the inherent dynamism of the American economy play itself out. Deficit worries are also often accompanied by calls for higher taxes rather than lower spending. Supply-siders cite the trade and budget deficits under [President Ronald] Reagan, pointing out that the sky did not fall in the 1980s and massive growth occurred.

Still, the most public faces of the supply-side movement accept some sort of deficit reduction plan. In his latest otherwise laudatory book, *Bullish on Bush*, the Club for Growth's Stephen Moore calls the current budget deficits "inexcusable," and jabs sharply that Republicans "no longer have a credible anti-big government agenda." Moore also quotes the libertarian Nobel Prize–winning economist Milton Friedman, declaring the budget deficit "the single greatest deterrent to faster economic growth in the United States today."

"We have a budget process that works as well as a pub that opens its doors to a pack of fraternity brothers and tells them the drinks are on the house," Moore writes.

Most conservatives see the current spending outrages as a problem of collusion between moderate Republicans and liberal Democrats. Such dereliction of duty by wide swaths of the Republican Party has convinced [Congressman Mike] Pence, Ryan, and others that the conservative mandate of election 2004 should apply to reforming the system broadly, not just to quibbling over one bill or another. Whether talking about tax reform, budget reform, or Social Security reform, the central theme amongst them is "fundamental change."

"When it comes to spending, it's not bad people," Pence said. "It's bad process. If anyone believes we can restrain federal spending without fundamentally altering procedure, well, frankly, that is just not going to happen."

Government Reform Is Needed to Control Spending

It is an article of faith among House conservatives that entitlements must be reformed in order to save them and that the best method of combating out-of-control federal spending is first to change how the government works on the budget. Rep. Ryan has authored, along with fellow conservative Texas

Republicans Clash Over "Pork-Barrel" Spending

[Oklahoma Senator] Tom Coburn recalls a confrontation on Capitol Hill shortly after last November's [2006] GOP bloodbath. He ran into his fellow Republican Senator Ted Stevens of Alaska, the then-powerful chairman of the Senate Appropriations Committee and chief Senate sponsor of the Alaska Bridge to Nowhere. "He strolled up to me and said: 'Well, Tom, I hope you're satisfied for helping us lose the election.'" Stevens was evidently still infuriated by Coburn's nationally publicized crusade against runaway pork-barrel spending over the past two years. To that, Coburn, never the shrinking violet, replied: "No, Ted, you lost us the election."

The story speaks volumes about the sad state of affairs inside the Republican Party and the Gulf of Mexico–sized disconnect between the party powerbrokers in Washington and a thoroughly disgusted conservative base. The party regulars still blame the November [2006] defeat on the fiscal whistleblowers like Coburn, not the fake Republicans who grew a $1.9 trillion budget by an additional trillion dollars in five years.

Stephen Moore, "Pork Buster in Chief,"
American Spectator, *August 23, 2007.*

Rep. Jeb Hensarling, the Budget Fraud Elimination Act, which seeks to overturn much of the Budget Act of 1974, a bill passed by a Democratic majority and signed by a hamstrung Richard Nixon, grasping at liberal straws in the final month before his resignation. The act ushered in the era of massive, pork-filled omnibus spending bills, even larger deficit spending, and general unaccountability.

The federal budget today is passed as a resolution, a mere set of guidelines for spending that can be easily ignored. Ryan's bill would give the federal budget the force of law, and any "budget busting" requests would require approval by a two-thirds majority. It would also close the grossly misused "emergency spending" loophole and send any savings from spending cuts back to the U.S. Treasury instead of back to the Appropriations Committee, where it currently goes to be re-spent.

"Right now you can find the most egregious boondoggle in a bill and eliminate it, but you can't save that money," Ryan said. "It goes back into the pork pot to be spent somewhere else. Nothing is accrued to savings. The money is spent at all costs."

This is not, however, the first time congressional budget restraint measures have been employed. The Gramm-Rudman bill, for example, was enacted in 1985 to reduce the $200 billion budget deficit. (Ironically, President [George W.] Bush is now promising to cut the record 2004 deficit of $417 billion in half by the time he leaves office in 2008—in other words, cut it down to roughly 1985 crisis levels. The U.S. budget deficit for last November alone was almost $58 billion.) Gramm-Rudman required automatic spending cuts if Congress exceeded spending caps. Accordingly, the deficit fell from 6 to 3 percent of GDP [gross domestic product], government spending dropped from an annual growth rate of 8.7 percent to 3.2 percent, and entitlement spending slowed to a rate of 5 percent. As further proof of its effectiveness, unions, tax-and-spend liberals, and all the other usual suspects were furious.

Previous Success Controlling Spending

The good news was that by 1990, when the law was repealed, the deficit had been cut by 40 percent. The bad news was that Congress had decided they couldn't live by such rules, a fact that does not bode particularly well for the current crop of reformers.

Fiscal conservatives disappointed with the results of the last four years [2001–2004] should know that time hasn't been entirely wasted, Ryan said. "This isn't a one-year or a two-year fight," he noted. "We've been on the move for a while. You have to lay groundwork for any transformational legislation." Losing a battle, he said, is sometimes necessary to advance an issue. Ryan and his supporters brought the Budget Fraud Elimination Act forward last summer [2004] and lost. They knew they were going to lose, but they wanted to get politicians on the record against fiscal common sense before the election.

"We brought forward the most comprehensive version of budget reform I've ever seen, broke it into 11 distinct policies, and made members vote on each section," Ryan said. "Our suggestions might sound like common sense to people outside of D.C., but there are representatives who consistently vote against this stuff. It's stunning."

Dick Armey, who fought similar battles in those same trenches, is skeptical about Republicans betting so much on procedural reform. "Policy reform is a lot easier than process reform," he said. "Policy is about real people in the real world, and it's much easier to explain to constituents. Congress is an unreality, a world carefully constructed to protect the interests of its members. Getting a majority of members to go along with rule changes that will make their life harder will be tough, especially since it will mean defying the appropriators to some degree. They've got idealism on one side, and the appropriators have got dollar bills on the other. That's a tough fight."

Not Rocking the Boat

Armey hopes battles for fundamental Social Security and tax reform, which suddenly appear politically winnable, are taken up first. Linda Killian, author of *The Freshmen: What Happened to the Republican Revolution?*, a fascinating chronicle of the 1994 Republican House takeover, considers the idea of a new Republican revolution overblown.

"I don't see the same sort of revolutionary fervor in the Republican Party about ending deficits as I did in 1994," she said. "Back then it was as if conservatives were possessed. They were on a mission to balance the budget and reduce the size of government. They'd go to war with Republican leadership just as soon as anyone else if the leadership wasn't acting conservative enough. They were so serious they made Bill Clinton serious about it. So far today's Republicans have not been willing to press Bush in the same way."

Killian said that even the 1994 "revolution" didn't translate into long-term fiscal conservative votes.

"Even the '94 guys who are still around have lost their edge," she said. "The '94 Republicans, statistically, voted in favor of the prescription drug bill, the biggest entitlement since the 1960s, at the same rate as any other group. The realities of being in Congress, of trying to move up and get re-elected, have all sunk in, and many of those who have stuck around have obviously decided to not rock the boat." . . .

"Congress cannot sustain a Republican majority without an enthusiastic base," Pence said. "If we do not work towards the solutions we have been promising, it will the midterm election for us. Those are base elections, and the majority of our base is people who voted for us to see fiscal discipline in D.C. We abandon those folks at our own peril." . . .

"If we live up to our ideals, we'll prosper," Pence said. "If we fail, we run the risk of demoralizing millions of our most ardent supporters. It's like Yosemite Sam always used to say, 'Time's a wasting.'"

> "Bush has shown no leadership on
> spending reform—and Republicans
> have rebuffed even the mildest criti-
> cisms of their spendthrift ways."

The Republican Party Has Shown It Cannot Control Spending

Nick Gillespie and Veronique de Rugy

*Nick Gillespie is the editor-in-chief of the libertarian magazine
Reason. Veronique de Rugy is a research fellow at the conservative think tank the American Enterprise Institute. In this viewpoint, they compare the level of federal government spending under President George W. Bush and the Republican Congress to
the spending of other administrations. They show that Bush has
increased expenditures drastically, mostly on defense items but
also in nondefense discretionary, or optional, areas.*

As you read, consider the following questions:

1. What is "discretionary spending"? What programs fall
   into this category of spending?

Nick Gillespie and Veronique de Rugy, "Bush the Budget Buster," *Reason*, October 19,
2005. Copyright © 2005 by Reason Foundation, 3415 S. Sepulveda Blvd., Suite 400,
Los Angeles, CA 90034, www.reason.com. Reproduced by permission.

2. How much did the budget for the Department of Education grow in the five years (2001–2005) before the article was written?

3. According to the government, how much is the prescription drug bill expected to cost over ten years? Do the authors believe this figure is accurate?

The [George W.] Bush administration recently [October 2005] released its mid-session review of the federal budget for fiscal 2006. The new data reveal that in spite of repeated promises of fiscal responsibility by the Bush administration and congressional Republicans, things are bad and getting worse. After five years of Republican reign, it's time for small-government conservatives to acknowledge that the GOP has forfeited its credibility when it comes to spending restraint.

"After 11 years of Republican majority we've pared [the budget] down pretty good," [former House Majority Leader] Tom DeLay (R-Texas) crowed a few weeks back during ongoing budget deliberations. But nothing could be farther from the truth, at least since the GOP gained the White House in 2001. During his five years at the helm of the nation's budget, the president has expanded a wide array of "compassionate" welfare-state, defense, and nondefense programs. When it comes to spending, Bush is no Reagan. Alas, he is also no Clinton and not even Nixon. The recent president he most resembles is in fact fellow Texan and legendary spendthrift Lyndon Baines Johnson—except that Bush is in many ways even more profligate with the public till.

Mandatory Versus Discretionary Spending

The federal pie has two parts, each accounting for about 50 percent of outlays. "Mandatory spending" includes entitlement programs such as Medicare and student loans that are provided by law rather than by annual appropriations. Then there is discretionary spending, comprising most defense spending, homeland security, and programs such as farm subsidies and education. Discretionary spending is what the president and Congress decide to spend each year through appropriations bills. Because discretionary spending can theoretically be zeroed out each year, it is generally regarded as the clearest indicator of whether a president and Congress are serious about reducing government spending. Some major entitlement programs—most notably Social Security—are "off-budget," meaning they are not accounted for in either the mandatory or discretionary figures. . . .

Total real discretionary outlays will increase about 35.8 percent under Bush (FY2001–06)[1] while they increased by 25.2 percent under LBJ [Lyndon Baines Johnson] (FY1964–69) and 11.9 percent under [President Ronald] Reagan (FY1981–86). By contrast, they decreased by 16.5 under [President Richard] Nixon (FY1969–74) and by 8.2 percent under [President Bill] Clinton (FY1993–98). Comparing Bush to his predecessors is instructive. Bush and Reagan both substantially increased defense spending (by 44.5 and 34.8 percent respectively). However, Reagan cut real nondefense discretionary outlays by 11.1 percent while Bush increased them by 27.9 percent. Clinton and Nixon both raised nondefense spending (by 1.9 percent and 23.1 respectively), but they both cut defense spending substantially (by 16.8 and 32.2 percent).

Massive Increases in Spending

Bush and LBJ alone massively increased defense and nondefense spending. Perhaps not coincidentally, Bush and LBJ also shared control of the federal purse with congressional majorities from their own political parties. Which only makes Bush's performance more troubling. Like a lax parent who can't or won't discipline his self-centered toddler, he has exercised vir-

---

1. The "FY" stands for "Fiscal Year," the period from October 1 to September 30. Government expenditures are reckoned during this period rather than the normal calendar year.

George W. Bush Leads Recent Presidents in Increasing Discretionary Spending

Term	Total Discretionary	Non-Defense Discretionary	Defense
Lyndon Johnson	25.2%	21.4%	26.7%
Richard Nixon	−16.5%	23.1%	−32.2%
Ronald Reagan	11.9%	−11.1%	34.8%
Bill Clinton	−82.0%	19.0%	−16.8%
George W. Bush	35.8%	27.9%	44.5%

TAKEN FROM: Veronique de Rugy and Nick Gillespie, "Bush the Budget Buster," *Reason Online*, October 19, 2005.

tually no control whatsoever over Congress. In the wake of massive new funding for the Gulf Coast in the wake of Hurricane Katrina, Bush did timidly suggest that some of the new money be matched by reductions in pork projects embedded in the just-passed transportation bill. The Republican response to such efforts is summed up by Alaska Rep. Don Young's reply to critics of a $223 million "bridge to nowhere" in Ketchikan. Proponents of budgetary "offsets" can "kiss my ear," Young told the *Fairbanks Daily News-Miner*, adding that paying for Katrina-related measures by trimming transportation pork is "the dumbest thing I've ever heard." . . .

When confronted by its spendthrift ways, the Bush administration argues that much of the increase in nondefense spending stems from higher homeland security spending. It's true that most homeland security spending is tallied under nondefense discretionary spending. Yet when homeland security spending is separated out, the increase in discretionary spending is still huge: 36 percent on Bush's watch.

So only a part of recent increases are related to 9/11. And that's leaving aside the real question of whether even homeland security money—which has gone to pay for items such as Kevlar vests for police dogs in Columbus, Ohio—is being spent wisely. A substantial portion of Bush's increase in discretionary spending stems from new domestic spending initiatives. For a ready example, look no further than the Department of Education, one of three departments targeted for elimination by Republicans in 1994, when Tom DeLay and his budget-cutting friends first took control of Congress. In the last five years, Education's budget has grown by a stunning 79.9 percent.

Better on Mandatory Spending

If the performance of the president and Republican Congress is disheartening when it comes to discretionary spending, things look a little better when it comes to mandatory spending. Better, that is, than LBJ and Nixon. . . .

Total real outlays have increased by 23.4 percent under Bush, placing him second only to LBJ. As the architect of the Great Society, Johnson created vast new entitlements such as Medicare and Medicaid, which continue to balloon the mandatory portion of the federal budget. Mandatory spending reached its zenith under Nixon, partly because entitlement spending tends to balloon during recessions, as poverty rates and unemployment increase.

Because it is linked to the larger economy and reflects decisions often made before a particular president takes office, spending analysts tend to slight entitlement spending. Yet the president can still have a dramatic impact on entitlement spending. There's the LBJ example, where a sitting president creates new entitlements that drive up government spending. But there are other ways that a president can affect entitlement spending.

For instance, by cutting marginal income tax rates, an administration can substantially reduce the number of people unemployed and hence reduce entitlement payments. Also, the president can change the underlying laws that define how and to whom the money is distributed. President Reagan's first budget plan promised to "overhaul the nation's overgrown $350 billion entitlements system"; he also proposed numerous spending reductions to Medicare and Medicaid and was able to make some modest reforms to slow program growth rates. Those are some of the reasons why the total increase in mandatory spending during Reagan's first five years was a relatively paltry 12.4 percent. In 1996, President Clinton signed off on vigorous welfare reforms. Chief among them were the strong incentives for welfare recipients to get jobs, which benefited all Americans in the form of lower spending on welfare. The economic boom of the Clinton years—induced in part by large capital gains tax cuts—also worked to decrease entitlement spending.

Fiscal Recklessness

President Bush seems intent on following the LBJ model by making entitlement spending even more overgrown. In a fiscally reckless act, Congress and President Bush enacted the $550 billion (over 10 years) drug bill even though the budget is deep into deficit and Medicare already has a huge financing shortfall. Not only is the new drug program the biggest expansion in Medicare since its inception, it's virtually certain that the $550 billion price tag is a low-ball estimate. Despite the massive cost, some on Capitol Hill now want to expand these entitlements in the name of Katrina victims.

To date, the Bush administration has a disjointed, two-track budget policy. It has favored letting Americans keep more of their money via tax cuts while steadily building up the welfare state via unrestrained spending. Over time, that strategy can't work. As [economist] Milton Friedman and others have long argued, the size of government is found in its total spending and, ultimately, spending is a taxpayer issue. Higher spending and resulting deficits create a constant threat of higher taxes. It's no surprise that not just Democrats but even moderate Republicans are now arguing that Bush's recent tax cuts be allowed to expire.

The Republican Congress Shares the Blame

To be sure, Congress shares the blame for runaway spending in the past five years. Yet Bush has not vetoed a single spending bill during his tenure in office [as of October 2005]. To the contrary, he has signed every bill crossing his desk, including huge education, farm subsidy, and transportation bills. He has made only the most feeble efforts to rein in pork-barrel spending or offset new programs with cuts in existing ones.

What makes this all the more frustrating is that Bush, unlike Reagan and Clinton, faces a Congress that is controlled by his own party, which claims to be dedicated to smaller, more efficient government. Yet Bush has shown no leadership on spending reform—and Republicans have rebuffed even the mildest criticisms of their spendthrift ways. It seems incontestable that we should conclude that the country's purse is worse off when Republicans are in power.

> *"Most conservatives want to cut spending because they desire a government that is smaller in scope."*

Spending Can Be Controlled Only by Cutting the Size of Government

Ramesh Ponnuru

In the following viewpoint, Ramesh Ponnuru asserts that conservatives want to reduce spending in order to limit the size of government. Unfortunately, the more conservative of the two main political parties, the Republicans, have lost their passion for cutting spending. Ponnuru believes that to regain that passion, they must refocus on the long-term goal of a much smaller federal government. Ponnuru is the editor of the right-leaning magazine National Review.

As you read, consider the following questions:

1. What does Ponnuru believe is the best short-term strategy for achieving budget cuts?

2. Why does Ponnuru believe that to save money it is better, in the long term, to abolish programs than to take small cuts from every program?

3. What are some examples of indirect strategies to limit spending and the growth of government?

Many conservatives have been warning Republicans that they are throwing away their reputation as the thrifty party. But this isn't much of a threat. There are a lot of voters who would like lower spending, but there are few voters for whom it is a priority. Many people are willing to base their votes on getting a tax cut. Not many people vote in order to get a spending cut.

The politics of pork illustrates the point. Conservatives are now calling on congressmen to give up pork for their districts to pay for hurricane relief [in the aftermath of hurricane Katrina, September 2006]. Most congressmen get reelected with large enough margins that they could give up that pork and survive politically. But there are very few congressional districts where turning down a new bridge would actually gain a congressman votes. If that weren't the case—if there were large numbers of voters who cared intensely about cutting government spending—we wouldn't have the gargantuan federal establishment we do.

That is why [George W.] Bush did not run as a budget-cutter. Conservatives can justly claim to be surprised at the magnitude of the change in federal spending under Bush, but we cannot claim to be surprised at its direction.

Budget Process Needs Reform

What's worse is that even those voters who care about runaway spending don't have much interest in reforming the process by which Congress writes the budget. That process, set up near the high tide of congressional liberalism in 1974, is designed to maximize federal spending. Trying to keep spending

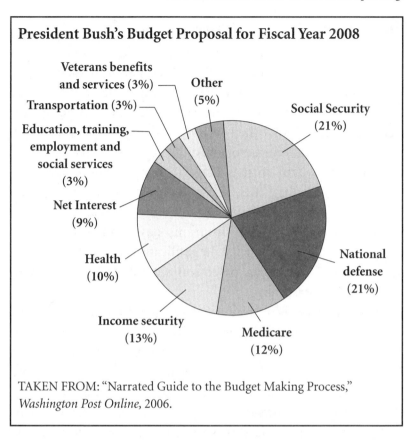

President Bush's Budget Proposal for Fiscal Year 2008

Veterans benefits and services (3%)

Transportation (3%)

Education, training, employment and social services (3%)

Net Interest (9%)

Other (5%)

Social Security (21%)

Health (10%)

National defense (21%)

Income security (13%)

Medicare (12%)

TAKEN FROM: "Narrated Guide to the Budget Making Process," *Washington Post Online*, 2006.

down without changing the rules is a fool's errand. The rules make it possible to keep spending under control for one year or even for a few years—if one is willing to invest a lot of political resources into the effort. But all that work is almost guaranteed to be undone before too long.

[Budget analyst Brian] Riedl explains how a genuinely effective spending limit might work. The House would have to change the rules so that a congressman could raise a "point of order" whenever legislation threatened to break that limit— and a super-majority vote would have to be required in order to allow the increase. The only problem with that idea: "You're never going to have grassroots rallies for point-of-order reform." . . .

Short-Term Strategy: Across-the-Board Cuts

In the short run, the most achievable spending cut is probably some kind of even, across-the-board reduction in spending on everything but defense, homeland security, and entitlements. A number of congressmen are calling for that, although the percentage reductions they seek vary. Congress has had regular and recent experience of making such cuts to reach the desired numbers, and so it is likely to happen. Since conservatives want spending cuts, since Republicans are in no great position to say no, and since going after particular programs is difficult because those programs have constituencies, an across-the-board cut is what Republicans should do now. But conservatives' long-term objectives should go beyond saving money in this fashion.

Conservatives want to cut federal spending in part because they think it would be good for the economy. But more than that, most conservatives want to cut spending because they desire a government that is smaller in scope. By this, they primarily mean one that attempts to perform fewer functions. The level of spending is a proxy for the size of government. But it is a very imperfect proxy. Spending can go up when the government stays within its proper boundaries, as when the government is fighting Nazi Germany. Spending can go down while the government is growing in other ways, e.g., through regulations. It would be worse than pointless if conservatives succeeded in cutting spending at the price of accepting more regulation, since the latter, being relatively hidden, is more insidious than the former.

Abolishing Programs

If the long-term goal is limiting government, then it would be better to abolish programs than to cut them. This is true even if you could save more money by cutting a lot of programs than by eliminating a few of them. Programs, once cut, can grow again more easily than programs, once abolished, can be revived. It is largely pointless to try to abolish cabinet departments, as the Gingrich Congress tried to do, since the likely consequence would be merely to shift programs from one department to another.

Conservatives have not devised any plan to shrink the government over time that inspires great confidence. Direct attempts to rein in the government, as in 1995–96, have not been sustainable. We are left with indirect strategies: for example, changing tax, health, and Social Security policies in the hope of shifting American politics rightward and making it possible to shrink the government in the future.

This strategy involves higher risks and higher rewards than an effort to keep spending as low as possible in the short term. If one wanted to try to keep government spending from growing from one year to the next, one might very well have favored [former Democratic presidential candidate] John Kerry last year [2004] on the theory that congressional Republicans would be tougher on his budgets than on Bush's. Someone trying to follow the long-run strategy to cut government—such as [conservative activist Grover] Norquist—would, on the other hand, have favored Bush in order to have a chance at Social Security reform and the like. The ambitious strategy, in other words, may lead to higher spending in the short run, but the long run may never come.

My own judgment is that conservatives are not capable of holding the line on spending in a series of short runs without maintaining the long-term goal, however distant, of a much smaller federal government. That goal must therefore be worked toward and juggled with other priorities, such as maintaining a strong defense and imposing restraint on the judiciary.

> *"Public investments and incentives to boost science, technology, innovation, education, and skills are central to fueling a high-powered knowledge economy. Yet public investment in knowledge has been falling."*

A Left-Leaning Strategy Would Use Government Spending to Spur Growth

Will Marshall and Robert Kuttner

In this viewpoint, Will Marshall, the president of the Progressive Policy Institute, and Robert Kuttner, editor of The American Prospect, *make the case for increasing government spending. Investing government money, they believe, in education, research, and technology infrastructure will help economic growth and thus increase the tax base. In addition, programs to help working families could give incentives for less well-paid people in America to save for their retirement or their children's education. How-*

ever, the authors believe the budget should be balanced, a goal they think could be achieved by cutting handouts to large corporations and by revising the tax code to make the wealthy pay a greater share.

As you read, consider the following questions:

1. How much do the authors claim would be saved by raising taxes on the wealthiest families and reinstating the inheritance tax?
2. What do the authors believe the government must do to improve the United States' position in world trade? Are they for trade restrictions?
3. What are three things the government can do to help workers who have to change jobs in the increasingly volatile new economy?

If liberals and New Democrats sometimes seem like the Hatfields and McCoys of center-left politics, it is because we each believe passionately that America's progressive soul is worth fighting for. For the most part, these debates within the family reflect principled disagreements about the best strategy for achieving both a just society and a progressive majority that embraces it. But though we still may disagree about some details, after years of radically conservative dominance of national politics, we find ourselves in vehement agreement with a simple proposition: The radical right is closing avenues of opportunity to working Americans.

This right-wing dominance, however, has produced a new unity on the progressive side. In this spirit, a group of us has gathered under a flag of truce to work out an alternative to Bushonomics: a progressive growth strategy for expanding the middle class.

Our progressive growth strategy aims at redressing today's imbalance between economic innovation and economic opportunity. It has four main elements.

Return Fiscal Sanity to Washington

As we learned in the 1990s, restoring fiscal discipline is integral to sustained economic growth as well as responsible government. It drives interest rates down, giving consumers and businesses the equivalent of a tax cut while also encouraging private investment. Let's start by rolling back the Bush tax giveaways to families earning more than $200,000 a year while protecting the tax cuts for middle- and low-income families. Then let's reinstate the inheritance tax, with a higher exemption for family farms or small businesses. These steps would save roughly $550 billion over the next 10 years while shifting the tax burden back from working families to the wealthy. And with an estimated $200 billion a year lost to tax cheating, a long overdue crackdown on tax-evading corporations and high-bracket individuals could capture a healthy chunk of this fugitive revenue.

The right has done almost as much damage on the spending side of the national ledger as the tax side. No one doles out pork like the GOP [Grand Old Party, a nickname for the Republican Party]: The recently passed transportation bill was larded with 3,251 "earmarks"—money added specifically for a particular member's state or district, or a special interest. This compared with just 538 in the 1991 highway bill. An important energy bill now languishes in Congress, in part because it was originally freighted with $31 billion in tax breaks for the oil, gas, coal, and electrical industries. No wonder even *The Wall Street Journal* editorially charged Bush with presiding over "the most profligate Administration since the 1960s."

To stop the pork spree, we'll need to restore real budget controls—including stronger versions of the "pay as you go" rules that effectively constrained spending and tax cuts in the 1990s—as well as budget caps. We should particularly crack down on corporate welfare—billions in tax breaks and spending programs for companies that don't need or deserve government handouts.

Hurricane Katrina Makes Infrastructure Deficit Apparent

If Americans woke up to see our country looking like the most afflicted of Third World nations [after Hurricane Katrina in 2005], it's no accident that it happened on the watch of an Administration that has determinedly cut spending on social services and infrastructure. The Bush Administration denied the Army Corps of Engineers request for $105 million for hurricane and flood protection for New Orleans last year—cutting it down to about 40 percent, leaving the levees that burst unrepaired because they didn't want to spend the money to get the job done. And this same Administration decided to try to make its tax cuts for the wealthiest citizens permanent, even as New Orleans drowned and Baghdad burned.

Ruth Conniff, "Drowning the Beast,"
The Progressive, *November 2005.*

Don't Starve Government, Feed Innovation

Restoring fiscal discipline in Washington is a necessary precondition for reviving broad prosperity in America. But it is not by itself an agenda for growth. As the next administration reduces long-term deficits, it must also find money for public investments we need to stimulate innovation and the creation of good jobs.

The right wants to put money in people's pockets by socking the next generation with a huge national debt. Progressives should do it the old-fashioned way—by helping Americans earn more of it through more productive jobs.

In today's economy, knowledgeable people—including entrepreneurs, skilled workers, cutting-edge researchers, and innovative companies—are the drivers of growth. In a global marketplace, our economy increasingly must specialize in higher-skilled, knowledge-intensive production. The 21st-century economy grows not because we do more of the same but because we do things differently and better.

Government has a vital role to play in stimulating growth in the digital age. Strategic public investments in research, education, and new-economy infrastructure like broadband and smart highways, as well as energy independence, are essential to sustaining a culture of innovation and strong institutional supports for technological change. Government must promote free and fair competition by protecting the fruits of U.S. research from intellectual-property theft overseas, by opening markets so that U.S. businesses and workers can sell their products to countries that are happy to export to us but want to keep their own economies closed, and by toughening enforcement of trade agreements as well as labor and environmental standards. It's also essential that the rich countries get serious about reducing subsidies and trade barriers that deny developing countries opportunities to export and grow.

Public investments and incentives to boost science, technology, innovation, education, and skills are central to fueling a high-powered knowledge economy. Yet public investment in knowledge has been falling. As a share of the GDP [gross domestic product], government support for basic research has declined under the Bush administration. We need major new investments in science and research, for example, an additional $10 billion per year in the advanced cyber-infrastructure program, industry–university research alliances, advanced manufacturing techniques, and a more robust National Science Foundation.

In the 1950s, Washington launched the interstate highway system, a network infrastructure for the postwar industrial economy. It's time to make a similar national commitment to build the network infrastructure of the knowledge economy:

the "last-mile," broadband, high-speed telecommunications infrastructure in the home. There's no reason, other than lack of leadership, that America should lag behind nations like South Korea and Canada in the broadband quest. We should set a national goal of getting truly high-speed broadband into 75 million homes over the next decade.

It's also time for serious new initiatives that will lift the skills of American workers—for example, through regional partnerships that would bring companies, labor unions, and public agencies together to set up new training systems for skills that are actually in demand.

Reform the Tax Code for the Benefit of Working Families

Besides rolling back the Bush tax cuts for the rich, progressives should launch a comprehensive effort to simplify a tax code larded with confusing, overlapping, inequitable, and sometimes ineffective deductions, credits, and other breaks. For example, we could consolidate 25 existing tax incentives into just four provisions aimed at expanding middle-class opportunity: a college-opportunity credit for any student attending college or graduate school; a single-family credit to replace four current provisions (including the child-tax credit and the Earned Income Tax Credit) and more assistance to families than all of them combined; a universal pension account that would give all workers an incentive to open a pension savings account and take it with them from job to job; and a refundable tax credit for new homeownership that all taxpayers, not just those who itemize, could take.

The current tax preferences are skewed upward. The highest-income executives get the most tax subsidies for their pensions. The most lavish homes generate the most extensive mortgage interest deductions. By revising these tax preferences downward, we could use tax policy to help working Americans get a foot in the middle class and give middle-class families the relief they deserve.

Expand the Economic Winners' Circle

Today's knowledge-based global economy presents us with a paradox: Growing opportunity seems inextricably linked to growing job volatility. This is particularly true as the information-technology revolution and cheap telecommunications continue to transform companies, work, and professional relationships, eliminating jobs through automation and enabling many others to move, either to lower-cost locations in the United States or, increasingly, overseas.

We can't turn back the clock to a time when workers could look forward to lifetime careers at a single company (or even industry). What we can do instead is reduce the tax incentives for inefficient economic activity motivated by tax avoidance and equip working Americans with a new set of tools they need to cope with change, manage risks, and take greater control over their own career security. There's a vital principle of equity here: How can we ask workers to brave the new rigors of global competition when corporate CEOs [chief executive officers] get golden parachutes even after running their companies into the ground? This new social compact should offer all U.S. workers lifelong access to career training, provide more effective public support for workers in transition, and allow more workers to secure an equity stake in their company and become owners of financial assets generally. We should create generous retraining funds for workers who lose their jobs through no fault of their own and modernize the unemployment insurance system to cover more part-time and low-wage workers and pay for skills upgrades. . . .

A Choice for Economic Democracy

Maybe we should take [presidential adviser] Karl Rove seriously when he draws analogies between the Bush White House and the McKinley administration, which cemented a GOP alliance with big business that lasted until the progressive triumph of 1912. We knew there was something atavistic about the Bush Republicans' vision; we didn't know it looked so far back, past Ronald Reagan to the GOP political economy of 1904, when the wealthy paid almost nothing in taxes, government provided little in the way of services or public-health and safety regulation, workers lacked economic power, and corporations, protected from foreign rivals, could wield their market power with impunity.

One thing is clear: Bush received no popular mandate in 2000 for such a radical and reactionary project. Many in his own party reject his program. Americans today face a stark choice—between plutocracy and economic democracy, between policies that entrench privilege and policies that expand middle-class opportunity. For all of us who call ourselves progressive, that's a no-brainer.

> "*Continued neglect of key social needs will be more harmful to the economy and society than a large deficit.*"

Fiscal Discipline Is Compatible with Meeting Spending Needs

Dean Baker and Heather Boushey

In this viewpoint, Dean Baker, codirector of the left-leaning Center for Economic and Policy Research, and Heather Boushey, a senior economist with the Joint Economic Committee of Congress, make the case for more government spending on social needs. These needs include health care and child care, which are needed by an ever-growing proportion of the workforce. The authors recognize the need for deficit reduction, but they believe that social spending will increase the overall welfare of American citizens.

As you read, consider the following questions:

1. How much higher is the level of spending, in percentages, than the amount of revenue the government receives?

Dean Baker and Heather Boushey, "Exercise Fiscal Restraint," *In These Times*, July 14, 2004. Reproduced by permission of the publisher, www.inthesetimes.com.

2. How much more, per person, does the United States pay for health care than the average for rich countries? Do American health statistics reflect the extra spending?

3. According to the article, which "problem" spending is not really a problem?

The large budget deficits of the [Ronald] Reagan administrations and the current [George W.] Bush administration will make limiting the size of the deficit an unavoidable priority. While the [Bill] Clinton–era stock bubble has largely deflated, the dollar bubble that the Clinton administration actively promoted persists, as does the huge (and growing) trade deficit—the inevitable result of an over-valued dollar.

Economic Trouble Ahead

The exact course of the dollar bubble is impossible to predict, but no economist believes that the United States will be able to continue to indefinitely borrow $650 billion a year (6.0 percent of GDP [gross domestic product]) from abroad. A falling dollar will lead to higher inflation and declining living standards because imported goods will become increasingly expensive, which will seriously complicate economic policymaking.

Finally, at some point, the housing bubble will burst. The timing of this collapse is unpredictable, but it is likely to follow rising interest rates. There are good reasons for believing that it will collapse soon, but there also were reasons for believing it would collapse two years ago. The collapse of the housing bubble will not only decimate the construction industry, it will quickly end a massive wave of consumption fueled by mortgage refinancing and home equity loans. As a result, when the housing bubble does collapse, we will enter a recession, possibly a severe one.[1]

1. The housing bubble burst during 2006, followed by a significant increase in foreclosures and a crisis in housing-related markets.

Understanding this economic situation is important because it limits our ability to address pressing budget priorities. Most importantly, a government should always be able to use its tax and spending policy to fight short-term economic difficulties. For example, if the collapse of the housing bubble leads to a recession, the goal of deficit reduction (an important priority) should be temporarily abandoned in order to provide stimulus through new spending and tax cuts oriented at low- and middle-income families.

In addition to deficit reduction, the other top priorities . . . should be reining in an out-of-control defense budget and meeting a set of long-neglected social needs, most importantly by fixing the healthcare system and addressing the need for universal pre-kindergarten.

The size of the current deficit provides a real basis for concern even for those of us who are not deficit hawks. To fund the general budget (almost everything except Social Security and most of the Medicare program), the government currently takes in about $1,200 billion a year in revenue. The spending level is roughly 50 percent higher, or $1,800 billion a year. This deficit of $600 billion is equal to about 5.4 percent of gross domestic product (GDP). It is not necessary to balance the budget, but the deficit does have to be brought into a range of 3 percent of GDP to be sustainable. And the only way to reach that 3 percent is to implement tax increases and/or spending cuts in the range of $300 billion a year.

Taking back the Bush tax cuts goes a substantial portion of the way toward correcting this shortfall. Taking back the entire tax cut would raise close to $200 billion annually. Simply taking back the portion of the tax cut going to the richest 2 percent of families . . . would raise close to $100 billion a year. Other progressive taxes, notably a tax on financial speculation, could go far toward bringing the deficit into line.

In addition, defense spending must be seriously readjusted in order to close the budget gap. The Bush administration has

Government Programs Should Help the Working Poor

While higher-wage workers take for granted that their jobs come with employer-based benefits like health insurance, a retirement plan, and maybe some paid time off, just over one-in-five workers (22.1 percent) are in a bad job—a job that pays low wages and provides no benefits.

That's where government work supports—programs that ensure that families can access basics such as healthcare, childcare, food, and housing—are supposed to step in.

Heather Boushey, "Millions of Americans in Economic Battle to Make Ends Meet," Atternet, October 13, 2007.

increased the annual defense budget by more than $110 billion (1.0 percent of GDP), with virtually no debate whatsoever. The pursuit of the war on terrorism is a recipe for endless interventions and ever-larger military budgets, but it would be difficult to claim it is making the country more secure. . . .

Spending to Fix Health Care Required

Continued neglect of key social needs will be more harmful to the economy and society than a large deficit. Healthcare must be the top priority on this list. Already, nearly 70 million people go without healthcare insurance for at least some part of the year. This number is sure to grow as more employers drop coverage or, as is happening more frequently, drop coverage for dependents. Recent policy fixes, such as the expansion of Medicaid under the State Children's Health Insurance Program (SCHIP), did little to stem the rise in the uninsured. There are indications that the expansion of SCHIP may have only persuaded many low-wage employers to drop coverage for dependents altogether and encourage their workers to sign their children up for SCHIP instead.

But the problem is not the uninsured. The problem is that the U.S. healthcare system is broken, which has led to rapidly escalating costs and deteriorating quality of care. The United States pays more than twice as much per person than the average for rich countries, yet its healthcare statistics rank near the bottom. Unless the system is repaired—along the lines of a universal Medicare system—costs will continue to rise and the number of people without insurance or with inadequate insurance will grow.

Fixing the healthcare system and extending coverage should save money, even in the short run. For example, the country currently spends more than $200 billion a year on prescription drugs because the government gives drug companies patent monopolies. If drugs were sold in a competitive market, and the government funded research, the savings would be on the order of $120 billion a year. Savings on administrative costs and excessive doctors' salaries also could more than offset the cost of covering the uninsured.

Other Critical Social Needs

The other social need that desperately cries for attention is childcare. Most mothers now work outside the home. As a result, they need safe, enriching, and affordable childcare. Spending money to develop full-day pre-kindergarten, attached to the public school system, would not only aid parents juggling work and family, but it would help children succeed in school. Currently, only the lowest income children have access to subsidized childcare. Even the bulk of this group (around 85 percent) do not receive any funds. Yet, difficulties accessing childcare—and especially pre-school—is a problem that is felt by families far up the income ladder.

One other problem that should not be neglected, even if it may not require large outlays, is global warming. The consequences of global warming for the planet are enormous. Restrictions on emissions of greenhouse gases will probably be more important than budget dollars in dealing with the problem. But some spending on developing clean technologies, as well as adjustment assistance for displaced workers, will be essential.

Finally, it is important to note one item that does not need addressing—Social Security. The program is completely solvent for the next 50 years, as a new report from the Congressional Budget Office just confirmed. Nonetheless, the business community and some in the corporate media establishment would desperately love to see Social Security attacked—apparently in the belief that it gives too much money to retired workers. The public should have their hatchets ready for any politician who tries to steal their Social Security benefits, otherwise the corporate media and wealthy campaign contributors will become powerful enough to gut the program.

Periodical Bibliography

The following articles have been selected to supplement the diverse views presented in this chapter.

Jed Babbin	"Bush Embraces Status Quo," *Human Events*, January 29, 2007.
William F. Buckley Jr.	"The Impossible Reform," *National Review*, April 5, 2004.
Gail Russell Chaddock	"Budget Dems Say Deficit Hole Is Even Deeper," *CongressDaily*, September 20, 2006.
	"Domestic Cuts Signal 'Tipping Point' in Budget Politics," *Christian Science Monitor*, February 25, 2005.
Clive Crook	"The Rancor Dividend," *Atlantic Monthly*, January/February 2007.
Peronet Despeignes	"All Hail the Free-Lunch President," *Fortune*, January 24, 2005.
Mike Franc	"Democrats Offer Big-Government Response to Bush Budget," *Human Events* 63, February 12, 2007.
David R. Francis	"'Macho Politics' Leads to Costly Budget Impasse," *Christian Science Monitor*, December 10, 2007.
Robert Samuelson	"A Deficit of Seriousness," *Newsweek*, May 16, 2005.
Bret Schulte	"Why Bush's Budget Does Not Matter," *U.S. News & World Report*, February 18, 2008.
Paul M. Weyrich and William S. Lind	"The Next Conservatism," *American Conservative*, February 12, 2007.
Richard Wolf	"To Solve Budget Deficit Problems, Parties Need to Take Risks," *USA Today*, November 13, 2006.

CHAPTER 2

Do Governments Spend Tax Money Wisely?

Chapter Preface

Even people who believe in high levels of government spending note that sometimes public expenditure is inefficient or wasteful. Although some people attribute these missteps to government corruption, a variety of factors can lead to the unwise spending of taxpayer money. In some cases, programs designed to meet genuine needs have loopholes that allow the not-so-needy to benefit. In others, the government is just too far removed from where the money is spent to monitor the situation—this phenomenon affects federal spending especially. At times, the goal of fairness clashes with efficiency. Costs are spread over all taxpayers, making the consumption less noticeable. However, important interest groups benefit significantly, so politicians have little incentive to offend those groups seeking government help. Farm program spending and federal health care spending illustrate these problems.

Farm programs were originally designed to help family farmers in difficult times. Those farmers face substantial risks, such as crop-damaging weather or low market prices for their produce. To counteract that risk, to protect the nation's food supply from monopolization by a few large agribusinesses, and to maintain the American icon of the small farm, Congress has instituted a variety of subsidies to keep small growers in business.

It has proved difficult to implement a program that keeps large corporations from benefiting from these expenditures on agriculture, however. The political pressure to include them is strong. Therefore, today agribusinesses receive millions of dollars in subsidies, which ultimately hurt both American family farmers and producers in poorer countries who would like to export food to the United States. Some critics maintain, from experience, that political maneuvering causes subsidies to go mainly to the wealthy businesses and that these unfair spending programs should be cut entirely. Advocates of subsidies, however, point out that family farms do benefit from these programs and that the United States has a cheap and abundant food supply, which is worthwhile even if some money goes to large growers.

Concerns over efficiency and fairness also clash in federal health care spending. People who believe in federalism (the philosophy by which states and even municipal governments, rather than the federal government, should make most spending decisions) point out that conditions vary from state to state and city to city. What works in rural, sparsely populated Utah might not work in urban and dense Connecticut. Supporters of federalism say that letting states decide how to spend money for health care would allow adaptation and experimentation, and states could learn from each other which types of programs work best. On the other hand, advocates of national, federal-level health care programs see it as unfair that a person in West Virginia might not have access to the same benefits as someone in California, that a Minnesotan might be denied a treatment available to a New Yorker.

The issues of fairness and efficiency, federal spending versus state spending, and others are explored further in the viewpoints of this chapter.

> "It's not even necessary to be a human being to qualify as a farmer. One study found farm subsidies going to 413 municipal governments, 44 universities, and 14 prison systems."

Subsidies to Wealthy Agribusinesses Are Counterproductive

Mark Zepezauer

Mark Zepezauer is an author whose publications include The CIA's Greatest Hits *and* Take the Rich off Welfare, *from which this viewpoint is taken. In the following selection, Zepezauer outlines how much the federal government spends on agricultural subsidies. Justified as aid to family farmers, the bulk of this money goes to large agribusinesses. According to Zepezauer, the subsidies hurt more than just the federal budget. They raise the price of farmland, making it tough for real family farms to stay in business. Higher-priced farmland results in higher food costs for consumers. In addition, large corporate farms tend to use more pesticides and machinery than small family farms do, resulting in greater environmental pollution.*

As you read, consider the following questions:

1. Which U.S. states get the most agricultural subsidies? Is this due to economic or political reasons?

2. What does the author propose would be a simpler and cheaper way to end rural poverty?

3. How much do price supports and other agricultural policies cost consumers in higher sugar prices? Prices for dairy products? Peanut prices?

When agricultural subsidies began during the Great Depression, their main purpose was to keep farmers on the farm by enabling them to earn roughly what people in cities did. Of course, in those days, some 25% of the population lived and worked on farms. Today, only 2% of us do. These days the average net worth of farm households is $564,000—nearly double the $283,000 for nonfarm households. Farmers' household income from all sources (an average of $64,347 in 1999) has exceeded that of nonfarmers' income every year since 1986.

Subsidies Benefit a Wealthy Few

Agricultural subsidies are particularly bizarre these days because they go mostly to relatively few states, for relatively few crops, to benefit relatively few farmers. The wealthiest 10% of subsidized farmers take 74% of the handouts, while the bottom four-fifths get 12% of the total. The bottom half? Just 2%. And 60% of U.S. farmers get nothing at all. Five crops—wheat, corn, rice, cotton, and soybeans—receive 90% of all federal subsidies. Almost two-thirds of total U.S. farm production—including most fruits and vegetables—remains unsubsidized.

Concentrating the subsidies on certain crops also concentrates them geographically. Just 15 states receive 74% of the benefit from federal agriculture programs, while paying only 24% of the cost. In California, the largest agricultural pro-

Five States Received $33 Billion in Corn Subsidies Alone		
State	Subsidies 1995–2005	Percent of Total
Iowa	$9.94 billion	19.4%
Illinois	$8.26 billion	16.1%
Nebraska	$5.89 billion	11.5%
Minnesota	$4.95 billion	9.6%
Indiana	$3.97 billion	7.8%

TAKEN FROM: "Corn Subsidies for Wealthy Farmers," *Taxpayers for Common Sense, www.taxpayer.net.*

ducer, only 9% of the farms received any subsidy at all. (These were mostly big cotton and rice farms, while the state's many orchards and vegetable farms didn't get a penny.) The Northeast gets a particularly raw deal, paying for 30% of the cost of crop subsidies (that is, it contributes 30% of federal taxes), while receiving just 2.4% of the benefit. In an effort to get in on the party, New York's congressional delegation helped create a new subsidy for its dairy farmers in the 2002 farm bill.

Not surprisingly, many of the "luckiest" states are those that can help swing the results of national elections or that have powerful representatives in Congress who help to write farm legislation. The 2002 farm bill gave the most money to Iowa, and the largest increase to Texas. Iowa is the home of Senator Tom Harkin, then the chair of the Senate Agriculture Committee. And Texas sent Republican Larry Combest, chair of the House Agricultural Committee, and Democrat Charles Stenholm, a member of the same committee, to Washington, where they helped double the amount of subsidies for their home state.

Payments to Politicians

And just coincidentally, Representative Stenholm himself is a subsidized farmer, receiving more than $39,000 under the

1996 farm bill (from 1996 through 2002). At least ten of his colleagues, including Senators [Charles] Grassley (R-IA), [Richard] Lugar (R-IN), and [Blanche] Lincoln (D-AR), are also on the dole. Representative Marion Berry of Arkansas (not to be confused with the former mayor of Washington, DC) took in more than $750,000 in subsidies between 1996 and 2002. Perhaps you will not be surprised to hear that Berry feels that federal farm subsidy programs are "woefully underfunded."

Not only is the U.S. Department of Agriculture (USDA) generous in its handouts to farmers, it's also quite generous in who it calls a farmer. Making a complete mockery of the supposed aims of the farm subsidies (to help keep 'em down on the farm), the USDA doled out almost $3.5 billion to recipients in urban zip codes between 1996 and 2001. Many recipients aren't even located in the same state as their farms. Among celebrity farmers (outside of Congress) are billionaire David Rockefeller, basketball star Scottie Pippen, broadcaster Sam Donaldson, tycoon Ted Turner, and corporate crime poster boy Kenneth Lay of Enron. In fact, any land that produces $1,000 or more in agricultural products can be officially regarded as a farm. So if you see the word "farmers" in quotes below, you'll know why.

Of course, it's not even necessary to be a human being to quality as a farmer. One study found farm subsidies going to 413 municipal governments, 44 universities, and 14 prison systems. And such Fortune 500 companies as Chevron Oil, John Hancock Life Insurance, Caterpillar Manufacturing, and Eli Lilly Pharmaceuticals are also quote, farmers, unquote—subsidized with your tax dollars. . . .

One last thing before we dive into the details. Despite all the booty being siphoned off to the wealthy, these programs are routinely justified by the need to help combat rural poverty or save small family farms. But there's an alternative that would be a whole lot simpler and cheaper. We could bring the income of every full-time farmer in the United States up to at least 185% of the federal poverty level (about $33,000) for just $4 billion a year. If the agribusiness subsidy's goal were to reduce rural poverty, we could simply write a check to every poor farmer. But of course that's not the goal anymore, is it? . . .

The "Cheaper Food" Ruse

One rationale for agribusiness subsidies—to the extent that they have any—is that you get cheaper food prices out of the deal. Dream on.

First of all, we pay for many of these handouts with our income taxes, so you'd have to add a portion of those taxes to your food bill to come up with an accurate total. According to one estimate, the average household can tack on $1,805 over the next decade. Besides that, there are indirect subsidies you pay for at the checkout counter without even realizing it.

Price supports, import restrictions, and market and production quotas keep the prices of sugar, dairy products, and peanuts higher in the United States than on the world market. They cost consumers $2 billion a year in higher sugar prices, $1.7 billion in higher dairy prices, and $500 million in higher peanut prices. That's $4.2 billion at the cash register right there.

But crop subsidies actually help drive up the price of many other foods, because they help inflate the cost of rural real estate—by some 25% in 2000 alone. Land that produces subsidized crops is worth more, thus bidding up the price of neighboring land. But more important, because subsidies are paid according to the number of acres planted (instead of farmer need), land becomes overvalued. Land prices are the single biggest contributor to the cost of food.

As a further illustration of the law of unintended consequences, the higher land prices are pushing more small family farms out of business and contributing to the dominance of corporate factory farms. Subsidies push up the price of land beyond what many poor farmers can afford. If they're tenant farmers, their rent goes up, and if they're owner-operators, their property taxes go up. Since neither group can afford to expand their operations, big corporations are able to gobble up more of the available land—which then makes the remaining land that much more valuable. On top of that, the larger agribusiness concerns bid up the price of land in competition with each other, leaving small family farms in the dust.

Even when agribusiness subsidies actually do bring down the cost of food, you typically end up paying for them in other ways. For example, diverting productive salmon streams to grow potatoes in the desert may be great for fast-food outlets and the corporate farmers who supply them, but it's hell on fishermen and recreational workers. Their unemployment insurance is part of the cost of your cheaper meal.

Subsidizing Environmental Destruction

The bottom line is that as agribusiness consolidation has increased, farm employment has declined. There have been jobs created in peripheral sectors, but not as many; employment in these sectors grew by 36,000 from 1975 to 1996, while farm employment dropped 667,000 jobs. More tellingly, the job "growth" in these sectors comes largely at the expense of the environment. Larger farms require more pesticides and machinery, leading to more pollution in our skies and streams as well as our food. So once again, we're subsidizing the deterioration of our environment, and we pay for it in health care costs as well as in taxes.

> "Members of Congress making pork-
> barrel spending promises to their con-
> stituents and delivering on them is one
> thing, but the buying and selling of ear-
> marks by private speculators . . . is
> quite another."

Lobbyists and Congressmen Collude to Waste Taxpayers' Money

Ronald D. Utt

Ronald D. Utt is a senior research fellow at the conservative Heritage Foundation. His work focuses on budget, privatization, housing, and transportation issues. In the following viewpoint, Utt criticizes congressional "earmarks," clauses that are attached to spending bills and guarantee that money will be spent in a representative's district or senator's state, or on a particular project. Utt makes the case that earmarks are driven by lobbyists. Earmarks allow these well-paid consultants to direct federal money to their private clients or municipalities that hire them.

Ronald D. Utt, "A Primer on Lobbyists, Earmarks, and Congressional Reform," *Heritage Foundation Backgrounder*, April 27, 2006, pp. 1–6. Copyright © 2006 The Heritage Foundation. Reproduced by permission.

In return, lobbying firms pay campaign contributions to Congress members, creating a cycle that encourages more spending and gives the appearance of corruption.

As you read, consider the following questions:

1. According to the Congressional Research Service, what was the increase in number of earmarks between 1994 and 2005?
2. What is one of the main reasons for the growth of earmarks?
3. Which article and section of the United States Constitution indicates who has the power to appropriate (spend) money? To whom does the Constitution give that power?

Two seemingly unrelated events in 2005 promise to contribute to some of the most significant changes in federal budget practices since the enactment of the Budget Control and Impoundment Act in 1973.

Waste and Corruption

First, the enactment of the Safe, Accountable, Flexible, Efficient Transportation Equity Act (SAFETEALU) in late July revealed that there was a limit to the congressional waste that the American public was prepared to tolerate. With its more than 6,300 pork-barrel earmarks, the federal highway program and Representative Don Young's (R-AK) $220 million for the infamous "bridge to nowhere" became objects of national ridicule. As the public demanded a remedy, many fiscally conservative Members [of Congress] intensified their efforts to curtail the embedded fiscal irresponsibility that has made pork-barrel spending increasingly commonplace.

Second, the indictment of former Representative Randy Cunningham (R-CA) for selling earmarks to defense contractors and the revelations of Jack Abramoff's unethical lobbying practices have added the taint of corruption to the earmarking process, which had once seemed merely irresponsible.[1]

Egged on by the national media, the public responded with a degree of disgust that initially forced worried Members of Congress to take a number of steps to appear responsive to the public's concern. Among these early steps was a dramatic request from Senator Ted Stevens (R-AK) that the Senate delete funding for the two controversial bridges in Alaska, though the governor decided to restore spending for them a month later. . . .

Congress Members Are Skeptical About Change

Yet despite the broad public concern, presidential interest, and the introduction of dozens of legislative remedies, most in Congress remain skeptical about the need for any change in behavior. In a radio interview, Senate Minority Leader Harry Reid (D-NV) said, "There's nothing basically wrong with the earmarks. They've been going on since we were a country." In response to the President's expression of concern, Senator Stevens retorted that "What needs fixing is to have the public understand what we do when we earmark bills." During his recent primary challenge, Representative Tom DeLay (R-TX) emphasized "that he can bring home pork. His handouts claimed more than $1 billion in federal dollars to Houston-area transportation projects, the port, NASA, universities and law enforcement." Of the transportation earmarks, DeLay said, "Quite frankly . . . [we're] using earmarks to force dollars into this region."

With their lucrative client contracts now at risk, the vast lobbying community is providing congressional skeptics and opponents of reform with vocal support and will certainly use its considerable skills, contacts, and resources to thwart any

1. Jack Abramoff was convicted of corrupting public officials and defrauding his clients, several Indian tribes, in January 2006.

Earmarks in Highway Reauthorization Bills, 1982–2005

Year of Bill	Earmarks
1982	10
1987	152
1991	538
1998	1,850
2005	6,371*

*"Table 1: Earmarks in Highway, Reauthorization Bills, 1982–2005,"
in "A Primer on Lobbyists, Earmarks, and Congressional Reform,"
Heritage Foundation Backgrounder, April 27, 2006, p. 4.
Copyright © 2006 The Heritage Foundation.
Reproduced by permission.*

meaningful reform that would undermine its prosperity. John Engler, head of the National Association of Manufacturers and former Michigan governor, testified in a Senate hearing that "Additional rules and laws weren't needed." At the same hearing, Paul Miller, president of the American League of Lobbyists, echoed a theme that will be at the core of the anti-reform defense effort in the coming months: "[T]his is not a widespread scandal. . . . Our government is not corrupt, lobbyists are not bribing people, and Members of Congress are not being bought for campaign contributions. . . . I don't think we can say with certainty that the current system is broken." . . .

The Growth of Questionable Practices

As Congress and the lobbying community scramble to defend themselves against charges of questionable practices and illegal influence peddling, many note—quite correctly—that the vast majority of Members and lobbyists are scrupulously honest, abide by all the rules, and are doing nothing more than exercising their constitutional right to petition government on behalf of themselves or their clients. Nonetheless, a growing body of evidence suggests that illegal and questionable lobbying practices are not uncommon and that incidents such as those involving Mr. Abramoff have likely been repeated in similar transactions between other lobbyists and Members.

A recent Congressional Research Service (CRS) analysis indicates the scope of such activities. The analysis found that the number of earmarks authorized by Congress in appropriations bills alone increased from 4,155 in 1994 to 15,887 in 2005—an increase of 282 percent. Using a slightly different methodology, Citizens Against Government Waste (CAGW) concluded that there were 1,439 earmarks in 1995, which grew to 13,997 in 2005, for an increase of 872 percent. By both the CRS and CAGW counts, earmarks in fiscal year (FY) 2006 fell by about 3,000, in large part as a result of the refusal of Senator Arlen Specter (R-PA) to allow any in the Labor–Health and Human Services bill.

Earmarking in federal highway reauthorization bills shows an even more dramatic longer-term trend. Notwithstanding Senator Reid's contention that "They've been going on since we were a country," . . . the data provided by the CRS and CAGW demonstrate that today's volume of earmarking is a relatively recent phenomenon.

Beach Resorts Favored over Flood Control

In large part, this escalation in the number of earmarks reflects the growing number of lobbyists offering to obtain them for a fee. As the number of earmarks increases with each passing year, the business attracts more lobbyists who apply more pressure on Congress to spend more on pork-barrel spending.

For example, the annual appropriations bill for the civilian programs of the Army Corps of Engineers typically is the most earmarked bill produced by Congress. The Corps' $5.3

billion annual budget for FY 2006 spawned a lucrative practice among lobbyists seeking a piece of the action for their paying clients. Among them is Marlowe & Co., which specializes in representing seaside resort communities seeking money from the Corps for "beach nourishment" projects. With the Corps' budget limited by annual appropriations, beach projects that promote tourism and enhance the value of vacation homes come at the expense of investment in flood control, including improved levees. . . .

Turning Pennies into Dollars

As the number of earmarks has escalated, there has been a similar increase in the number of lobbyists registered with the House and Senate, indicating their intentions to pursue clients' interests with the Appropriations Committees. According to a Knight-Ridder [news agency] article on lobbying, 1,865 lobbyists were registered with Congress in 2000 to pursue appropriations issues, but by 2004, the number is estimated to have increased to 3,523 lobbyists, an increase of 89 percent in four years. Even if Mr. Abramoff's activities were an aberration or a "not widespread" practice, 3,522 other lobbyists would still be registered to pursue earmarks for paying clients.

Adding to the pressure for earmark growth is lobbyists' increasingly common practice of aggressively marketing their services with unsolicited offers to prospective earmark buyers. This side of the business was exposed more than a year ago when officials in Culpeper County, Virginia, received an unsolicited offer of assistance to obtain a congressional earmark from Alcalde & Fay, a Washington-area lobbying firm. According to the public discussion of the offer at a subsequent meeting of the county's board of supervisors, a representative of the firm approached a county official with the offer to obtain an earmark of $3.5 million to construct a community sports complex in the county.

Although the county had planned to finance the complex with the proceeds of a county bond offering that the voters had already approved, the representative "expressed optimism that funds for the $3.5 million sports complex could be tied to one or more federal appropriation bills." "The cost of hiring Alcalde and Fay would be $5,000 per month, with an 18-month recommended contract." For a total fee of $90,000 in return for a prospective federal grant of $3.5 million, the lobbying firm was proposing to sell the county federal taxpayer money for just 2.6 cents on the dollar—something that was not really the firm's to sell. That the lobbyist believed he could deliver on the transaction indicates that something is terribly wrong in today's Congress.

Lobbyists Influence the Expenditure Process

Members of Congress making pork-barrel spending promises to their constituents and delivering on them is one thing, but the buying and selling of earmarks by private speculators as if they were bushels of wheat on the open market is quite another. Apparently, all this wheeling and dealing is taking place without any involvement (at least not yet) by a Member of Congress. Since Article I, Section 9, Clause 7 of the Constitution reserves the power of appropriating money from the U.S. Treasury exclusively to Congress, how is it that these lobbyists have come by the same privilege, and who has allowed it to happen? . . .

In defense of the lobbying practice, some contend that the lobbyists earn their fees because they are more adept at making an effective pitch to Members and staff on the importance of a project. Yet if that was all there was to it, why could the Culpeper County officials not simply visit with their Congressman when he or she was back in the district and make the request themselves? While many earmarks may in fact result from routine meetings between Members and constituents, the fact that so many petitioner/constituents pay tens of thousands of dollars for an alternative channel to the U.S. Treasury offers disturbing insight into the appropriations process and the extent to which parts of it have been outsourced to the K Street lobbyists in return for campaign contributions and other sorts of rewards and favors.

> *"For higher-quality and lower-cost government, traditional state and local activities should be moved back to the states."*

Moving Budget Decisions to the States Will Lead to Less Spending

Chris Edwards

Originally, the U.S. Constitution limited the role of the federal government, leaving most spending issues up to the states, according to economist Chris Edwards of the libertarian Cato Institute. In this viewpoint, Edwards documents the growth of federal spending in a variety of areas that were originally the preserve of state governments. Washington takes in money through a high level of taxation and determines, by means of federal "block grants," how money is spent at the local level. Edwards believes that money should be kept at the local level, where cities and states can control how much revenue to raise and how to spend it. This system would result in more efficient spending on local problems.

Chris Edwards, *Downsizing the Federal Government*, Washington, DC: Cato Institute Press, 2005. Copyright © 2005 Cato Institute. All rights reserved. Reproduced by permission.

As you read, consider the following questions:

1. From 1960 to 2005, how much, as a percentage of total federal spending, did grants to state and local governments increase?

2. Which president tried to cut federal grants to states and localities? Was he successful? Did the cuts last?

3. What is meant by the author's term "gold-rush response" to federal grant opportunities? How does this response lead to wasteful spending?

The federal government was designed to have specific limited powers, with most basic governmental functions left to the states. The Tenth Amendment to the Constitution states this clearly: "The powers not delegated to the United States by the Constitution, nor prohibited by it to the States, are reserved to the States respectively, or to the people." Unfortunately, the federal government largely ignored the Tenth Amendment during the 20th century and undertook a large number of activities that were traditionally and constitutionally reserved to the states.

The primary means that the federal government has used to extend its power are grants to state and local governments ("grants in aid"). Federal granting began during the 19th century, expanded during the 1930s, and ballooned during the 1960s. Some of the earliest federal grant schemes were for agriculture and highways. The Federal Aid Road Act of 1916, for example, provided federal aid to the states for highways on a 50-50 funding basis.

In the last two decades, there have been efforts to revive federalism and devolve activities such as education and highways back to the states. Under President Ronald Reagan in the 1980s and the Republican Congress of the mid-1990s, some federalism initiatives were pursued. But those initiatives were modest and short-lived, and the federal government has continued to grow, usurping ever more state and local activities.

Size and Scope of Federal Grants

In 2005 federal grants totaling $426 billion will be paid to lower levels of government for a huge range of activities, including education, health care, highways, and housing. Grants to state and local governments increased from 7.6 percent of total federal spending in 1960 to 17.2 percent in 2005.

The federal grant structure is massive and complex, as detailed in the 1,967-page "Catalog of Federal Domestic Assistance" [CFDA], available at www.cfda.gov. This publication is a comprehensive summary of federal grant programs to lower levels of government and private organizations. The CFDA lists 770 different grant programs aimed at state and local governments. Grant programs range from the giant $186 billion Medicaid to hundreds of more obscure programs that most taxpayers have never heard of. The CFDA lists a $16 million grant program for "Nursing Workforce Diversity" and a $60 million program for "Boating Safety Financial Assistance." One Environmental Protection Agency program hands out $25,000 grants to local governments for projects that "raise awareness" about environmental issues.

The huge size of federal granting activity has created an industry of consulting firms, computer software, and trade publications all geared to helping state and local governments win federal grants. But complexity, high administrative costs, and duplication have long been the bane of federal granting. In recent years, for example, spending for "first responders" such as firefighters has been popular, and there are 16 overlapping federal grant programs that provide such funding.

Overlapping Programs Create Waste

Federal grant programs not only overlap with each other, they overlap with the activities of state and local governments. The result, as political scientists have observed, is that the three layers of government in the United States resemble, not a tidy layer cake, but a jumbled marble cake. Federal expansion into state areas through grants has proven to be a wasteful way of governing the nation, and the federal grant empire should be radically scaled back.

Ronald Reagan tried to do just that. In his 1983 budget message, Reagan argued that "during the past 20 years, what had been a classic division of functions between the federal government and the states and localities has become a confused mess." Reagan tried to cut federal grants and to sort out the "confused mess" of federal and state activities. He had some success.... Between 1980 and 1985, Reagan cut overall grant spending by 15 percent in constant dollars and non-health grants by 21 percent. However, the cuts were short-lived, and grant spending increased rapidly during the 1990s....

The increase in federal grants has occurred because of political logic, not economic logic. Federal grants allow Washington to side-step concerns about expansion of its powers over traditional state activities. By using grants, federal politicians can become activists in areas such as education while overcoming states' concerns about encroachment on their activities by shoveling cash into state coffers. One observer in 1932 noticed that the federal government "bribes the states by federal subsidies to acquiesce in greater federal powers, and the consequent surrender by the states of their reserved powers." The losers are average Americans, who want quality government services at minimum cost but do not get them under the current federal-state structure....

Five Pathologies of Grants

A high-minded purpose may underlie federal grant programs, but grants are an inefficient method of governing America. The money to fund federal grants comes, of course, from taxpayers living in the 50 states. They send their tax money to Washington where it gets reallocated by Capitol Hill horse-trading and routed through layers of departmental bureaucracy. The depleted funds are sent down to state and local agencies, coupled with long lists of complex federal regulations to comply with. . . .

Five key pathologies of grants are discussed in turn here. The first pathology of federal grants is that they set off a gold-rush response in state and local governments, producing extravagant overspending, as Warren noted. State and local politicians gold plate their programs and spend wastefully because someone else is paying part of the costs and democratic accountability is more distant. As one extreme example of waste, the head of Maryland's Office of Crime Control and Prevention was indicted in 2004 for diverting federal grant money into a political campaign.

The gold-rush response is particularly acute with federal "matching" grants, under which state politicians can spend an added dollar while charging state taxpayers only a fraction of the cost. If a grant program has a matching rate of 50 percent, state politicians can expand a program by $2 million and taxpayers in their state will pay just $1 million more in taxes. Michael Greve of the American Enterprise Institute concludes that "federal funding has been the principal reason for the stupendous growth of state and local government over the past decades."

Unfair Distribution of Tax Dollars

The second pathology of grants is that they create unfair redistributions of taxpayer money between states. Federal highway grants, which total about $33 billion annually, illustrate the problem. The 50 states receive varying amounts of highway grants for each dollar of gasoline taxes sent to Washington. Some states have been consistent winners, and others losers, for decades. For 2003 the "return ratio" of highway money received to gas tax money paid ranged from 5.2 for lucky Alaska to 0.8 for unlucky Indiana. While some, mainly Southern, states lose out, other states get unneeded "highways to nowhere," often named after champion pork-barrel spenders such as Sen. Robert Byrd (D-WV) and former representative Bud Shuster (R-PA). It is no coincidence that the most massive highway project of recent decades, Boston's "Big Dig," was in the home of the former Democratic Speaker of the House, Tip O'Neill. . . .

Reduction of State Government Effectiveness

The third pathology of federal grants is that they reduce state government flexibility and innovation, while increasing state costs. For example, Davis-Bacon labor rules come as a package deal with federal highway dollars. These rules, which mandate the use of high-cost labor, increase highway construction costs by up to 15 percent. The most infamous federal highway regulation was the 55 mph national speed limit. It was enforced between 1974 and 1995 by federal threats of withdrawing state highway grant money.

Medicaid is burdened by perhaps the most inefficient federal regulations of any grant program. The Bush administration argues that the "complex array of Medicaid laws, regulations, and administrative guidance is confusing, overly burdensome, and serves to stifle state innovation and flexibility." But while the administration complains about Medicaid, its own No Child Left Behind [NCLB] education law of 2002 is the source of much state and local anger at top-down federal control. By 2005, 30 state legislatures had passed resolutions attacking NCLB for undermining states' rights.

Costly Bureaucracies

A fourth pathology of federal grants is the costly federal, state, and local bureaucracies that they require. Complex rules for grant application and administration are needed to keep track of the $426 billion that trickles down through the levels of government. To take one example, the $64 million Weed and

Seed anti-drug program for schools has a 74-page application kit that references 1,300 pages of regulations that grant recipients must follow. The Bush administration is right that the federal grant system is "overwhelming," "off-putting," and "intimidating." The administration has also concluded, not surprisingly, that grant programs are even less effective than other federal programs. . . .

Information Overload

A fifth pathology of grants is the time and information "overload" that they create for both citizens and federal politicians. Members of Congress fill their schedules with hearings, meetings, and press conferences on state and local issues. Members and their staff spend much of their time lobbying to steer pork projects from the 770 grant programs to their states and hometowns. House Speaker Dennis Hastert is a king at inserting earmarked projects into legislation for his home state of Illinois. But that results in his time being consumed by such activities as flying back to the state to attend dedication ceremonies for the pork projects he has secured. Hastert's parochial concerns mean that he has less time to deal with national concerns such as fixing mismanagement in the intelligence agencies.

For citizens, the overlapping agendas of federal, state, and local governments make it difficult to understand which politicians are responsible for which issues and programs. All three levels of government play big roles in areas such as transportation and education. That makes political accountability impossible. When programs fail, politicians simply point their fingers at other levels of government. Federal grants are a blight on responsible and transparent democratic government. . . .

New Federalism

For higher-quality and lower-cost government, traditional state and local activities should be moved back to the states.

That was the goal of the Reagan administration's "New Federalism" policies of the 1980s. Reagan wanted to re-sort federal and state priorities so that each level of government would have full responsibility for financing its own programs. For example, Reagan proposed that welfare and food stamps be fully financed and operated by the states.

Reagan sought to cut grants and terminate spending in areas that were properly state activities. He tried to abolish the Department of Education as an unwarranted boondoggle. Reagan also proposed "turnback" legislation to end federal highway funding and the federal gasoline tax that supports it. Another dimension of Reagan's plan was for the federal government to end funding to local governments and to deal just with state governments.

Reagan's New Federalism was only partly successful. He did manage to cut grant spending and turn some grant programs into block grants. In the Omnibus Budget Reconciliation Act of 1981, 59 grant programs were eliminated, and 80 narrowly focused grants were consolidated into 9 block grants. This consolidation into block grants substantially reduced the regulatory burden for those programs. As noted, real federal grants to the states were cut between 1980 and 1985.

The Republican Congress in the mid-1990s tried to revive Reagan federalism. It sought to abolish the Department of Education but was again unsuccessful. The Republicans did have some success in turning grant programs into block grants, most notably with welfare reform in 1996. However, President Clinton's veto pen was a barrier to many reforms, including the Republican budget plan for 1996 that would have turned Medicaid into a block grant and cut the program by $187 billion over seven years. . . .

With the large federal deficit, and with coming cost pressures in programs for the elderly, there is little budget room for spending on state and local activities. State and local governments are in a better position to determine whether residents need more roads, schools, and other projects. Shifting programs down to the states would better allow the diverse preferences of citizens to be realized. When states and localities are free to fashion services such as education independently, it is easier for people to see whether they are receiving value for their money because they can compare their government with the governments of neighboring jurisdictions. Federal policymakers should revive federalism, free the states, and begin cutting and terminating federal grants.

> *"Facing budget deficits, two of the nation's most populous states, California and New York, are proposing changes in Medicaid that could affect the eligibility of hundreds of thousands of people or decrease funding for hospitals, doctors, dentists, and pharmacists."*

Returning Spending Decisions to the States Leads to Inequalities in Health Care

Ron Scherer

In the following viewpoint, the author presents California and New York as key examples of states that were forced to make spending decisions and have chosen to cut into or alter their state's health care budget. According to the viewpoint, these proposed changes could affect a number of people, mostly low-income Americans. Ron Scherer is a staff writer for The Christian Science Monitor.

As you read, consider the following questions:

1. According to the viewpoint, how are some states responding to falling tax revenues?
2. About how many Americans are covered by Medicaid?
3. According to Ann Kohler of the National Association of State Medicaid Directors, why is there more flexibility in Medicaid than education?

L ow-income Americans, beware.

Facing budget deficits, two of the nation's most populous states, California and New York, are proposing changes in Medicaid that could affect the eligibility of hundreds of thousands of people or decrease funding for hospitals, doctors, dentists, and pharmacists.

Medicaid in Jeopardy Due to Cuts

Last month, California cut reimbursements to providers by 10 percent. With the legislature deadlocked over the budget, some healthcare facilities are now close to bankruptcy since no money is flowing to providers.

Other states are tacking on fees or cutting funds for charity care in hospitals. And, as more states face falling tax revenues, there could be more cuts by this fall.

"Medicaid is very much in jeopardy," says Iris Lav, deputy director at the Center on Budget and Policy Priorities in Washington.

The last time states were forced to cut Medicaid programs was after the 2001–02 recession when unemployment was high and tax revenues weak. At the same time, enrollment in Medicaid soared—rising 11 percent between 2000 and 2002 and another 7 percent in 2003. In 2006, the latest numbers available, spending on Medicaid hit $304 billion, up 48 percent from 2000.

One in 5 Americans is covered by Medicaid.

"This is a recurring problem states have during every recession," says Stephen Zuckerman, a healthcare economist at the Urban Institute in Washington. "Last time, Congress allocated more money."

This time, however, it might be more difficult to get federal aid, says Dan Hawkins, policy director for the National Association of Community Health Centers in Washington.

"There is good support for fiscal relief by several key members of Congress such as Rep. John Dingell (D) of Michigan," says Mr. Hawkins, who has watched the healthcare debate for 35 years. "But it all depends on whether Congress does a second fiscal stimulus package, and that is looking increasingly doubtful with President Bush saying he would veto any more fiscal stimulus."

When state lawmakers look at their budgets, the two largest expenditures are education and Medicaid. On average, states pay 43 percent of Medicaid costs, the rest picked up by Washington. However, solons are often loath to cut education funding, especially during the school year.

Instead, they start to look at healthcare.

"There is more flexibility in Medicaid than education," says Ann Kohler, director of the National Association of State Medicaid Directors in Washington. D.C. "You can define who to cover and how to set rates."

California's Case

That's what is happening in California. In February, the state, facing a growing budget deficit, announced a 10 percent cut in payments to providers, such as hospitals, doctors, and dentists. The cuts went into effect on July 1.

"Many doctors were forced to stop seeing new medical patients or in some cases existing ones," says Ned Wigglesworth, a spokesman for California Medical Association in Sacramento. "The reimbursement rate for a regular 15 minute visit was $24, which is below the cost of providing care," he says. "Now, it's gone to $21.60."

The Growth of the Medicaid Program

Legend for Chart

    A—Year

    B—Total Medicaid spending, state and federal,
      in billions

    C—Percentage of gross domestic product

A	B	C
1966	$1.3	0.2%
1976	$15.2	0.8
1986	$45.4	1.0
1996	$152.2	1.9
2005	$329.0	2.6

"Chart: The Growth of the Medicaid Program,"
Centers for Medicare and Medicaid Services.

Even with the reduction in rates, California still needed to find ways to bridge the chasm in its budget. So, in May, the state announced another series of changes, including a proposal to restrict eligibility from 107 percent of the federal poverty level to 61 percent.

Ms. Lav says there are estimates this could reduce the number of Medi-Cal (the state name for Medicaid) recipients by 400,000. "That means an adult making $14,500 a year, the equivalent of the minimum wage, would not be getting healthcare," says Mr. Wigglesworth.

The second round of potential changes have not gone into effect yet because the legislature has been deadlocked for the last 45 days over the budget. During that time the state has not made payments to providers.

"Some of the rural hospitals are on the edge of bankruptcy," says Jan Emerson, a spokeswoman for the California Hospital Association in Sacramento. "I had one rural hospital with 40 beds—39 of them for long-term patients—tell me they can go two more weeks before they have to shut their doors."

New York's Case

In New York's situation, Gov. David Paterson, facing a growing budget deficit, has proposed freezing Medicaid reimbursement rates for hospitals for the rest of 2008 and for 2009. Normally, the state factors in inflation.

In addition, Mr. Paterson wants to cut reimbursement rates by an additional 7.2 percent for the next two years and impose a new tax on hospital revenues. In New York City alone, this could result in a loss of $663 million in revenues, estimates the Greater New York Hospital Association.

"Some would have to cut back services, others would be forced to close their doors," warns Brian Conway, spokesman for the organization.

For Paterson, it could be difficult to convince legislators to make the cutbacks, which are also opposed by local 1199 of the Service Employees International Union, a powerful lobby in Albany.

"In the past, it is my understanding the unions have been quite successful at blunting cutbacks," says Mr. Hawkins. "This is a case where the traditional foes, the institutions and the workers are together on the same side and it multiplies the influence."

States Trying to Fund Shortfalls

The state of Maine recently added a $25 enrollment fee for adults for its Medicaid program. While the fee may seem small, Lav says it could strain low-income Down Easters faced with higher fuel costs and grocery bills. "It's amazing how hard it can be to come up with $25 when everything is going up in price," she says.

Other states, such as California and Arizona, are asking recipients to reenroll for benefits more frequently. New Jersey, also facing a huge budget deficit, has cut funds for charity care hospitals. And Florida has frozen reimbursements to nursing homes.

Some states with significant funding shortfalls are either waiting until after the election or studying how to bridge the gap. That includes Virginia and Mississippi.

In fact, some healthcare observers believe most states will wait until after the election to face up to their shortfalls. "Most states will pretend their budgets are in balance until November," says Lav. "It's hard to admit your budget is out of balance six weeks after you passed it."

> "Over the past two-plus decades, the tra-
> dition of local control has been shaken
> to its core, beset by a rash of state and
> federal mandates."

Local School Boards Should Have More Control over Education Spending

Glenn Cook

In the following viewpoint, Glenn Cook, the managing editor of the American School Board Journal, *claims that state and federal governments' controls on school spending are leading to a loss of community control. Pressed by national advocacy organizations, both the federal government and state governments have imposed targets on schools without providing additional funding. Some groups demand vouchers—money given directly to parents to spend on their children's education. Other national groups want a certain proportion of education funds spent in the classroom, for teachers and their expenses. According to Cook, such pressure is harming school boards', administrators' and teachers' ability to focus on educating students in the best way possible given local conditions.*

As you read, consider the following questions:

1. In how many states are school boards challenging the way schools are funded?

2. How many cents of every education dollar does the group First Class Education believe should be spent in the classroom?

3. According to business consultants Standard & Poor's, is there any one spending formula that will suit all of the nation's school districts?

Rae Waters had no reason to believe things would turn out like this. The Kyrene Elementary District, located in an affluent suburb in the Phoenix-Tempe area, was growing rapidly when she ran for the school board seven years ago. Buoyed by its proximity to Intel and Motorola, the 17,000-student district had a reputation as "the go-to place" for good schools.

But enrollment has dropped by almost 7 percent in the K–8 district over the past five years, and the number of Title I schools [those receiving federal Title I funds because of the students' poverty level] has climbed from two to five. The No Child Left Behind [NCLB] Act has brought attention to a growing achievement gap. Still, even as enrollment declined, expectations didn't—on the part of the schools or the parents.

When those expectations are different, as Waters has learned, the board feels the squeeze. In her case, the dispute was over schedule changes and cutbacks in electives at Kyrene's six middle schools, part of an effort to add more concentrated time in reading, writing, and math. In March—just three months after taking office as president of the Arizona School Boards Association—Waters faces a recall board election, and she remains perplexed by the entire affair. . . .

Local Control in Jeopardy

For boards and administrators, the long-term stakes are higher as well, perhaps more so than at any time since the school reform movement started. Over the past two-plus decades, the tradition of local control has been shaken to its core, beset by a rash of state and federal mandates, battles over consolidation and choice, and the growth of well-funded national organizations that have placed schools at the center of the political and culture wars. And parents, chafed by the loss of control, are taking out their frustrations on board members.

This constant friction, played out amid local politics, contributes to the belief that boards are unable or unwilling to do their job, when in all but isolated—and highly publicized—instances that's not the case.

"One of the dilemmas school boards face is that they have become the focal point of every single person with the latest fix for how to save children, and these fixes take on a million different forms," says William Howell, a Harvard University professor and editor of the book *Besieged: School Boards and the Future of Education Politics.* "There is a strong push for top-down control. At the same time, people want bottom-up accountability through parent choice, so everything is in flux." ...

The Money War

Nowhere is the struggle for power more pronounced than in the area of school finance. Anti-tax groups have pushed for caps on state spending to limit government growth, while districts in 45 of 50 states have filed court challenges over how schools are funded. Meanwhile, national initiatives such as the "65 cent solution," which would require districts to spend almost two-thirds of every dollar in the classroom, also are gaining traction in some regions.

"I'm not typically a guy who wakes up every morning worried about black helicopters looming overhead, but I believe this is all about finding reasons not to fund public schools," says Winston Brooks, superintendent of Kansas's Wichita Public Schools. "If it's not one strategy, it's another

States Battle the Federal Government over Education Funding

Fifteen states are conducting or have finished studies on the cost of complying with NCLB [the No Child Left Behind Act], according to the National Conference of State Legislatures (NCSL). Studies by Ohio and Texas estimated that the price to state taxpayers of complying with NCLB could run as high as $1.5 billion and $1.2 billion, respectively, each year.... Twenty-five states are considering or have passed resolutions asking Congress to fully fund NCLB....

Their challenges against NCLB increasingly are focused on one paragraph in the 1,100-page act—Section 9527 A—which prohibits the federal government from requiring states to pay any costs incurred by complying with the law.

Karan Peterson,
"No Letup in Unrest Over Bush School Law,"
Stateline.org, July 7, 2005.

strategy someone has uncovered. And it's all with the belief that if they can prove that schools are not spending money correctly, then we won't have to spend more money on them."

Arizona and Kansas are at the forefront of numerous education battles—political, financial, and ideological—that districts across the country face. Each has a Democratic governor and a Republican-controlled legislature with different agendas on how to resolve those battles.

"There is an ideological push to treat the public sector one way and the private sector another," says Becky Hill, [Arizona Governor Janet] Napolitano's education policy adviser. "You need to decide that education should be publicly funded and that there's a public expectation or there isn't. If you decide to fund the district and set goals, then you need to give local school districts the support and flexibility to achieve that goal."

The Community Is Losing Importance

In both states, consolidation and unification plans are being floated as a way to conserve resources and improve efficiency. Choice—in the form of open enrollment, charters, and vouchers—is being pushed, debated, or implemented at the state level. Arizona's legislature is expected to consider the 65 cent solution; Kansas lawmakers, who already have passed bills encouraging districts to use the model, are considering broader limits on government spending with the Taxpayer's Bill of Rights, similar to the Colorado initiative better known as TABOR.

"No Child Left Behind has, in many ways, circumvented school boards' authority, but governors are faced with the same problem," Noguera says. "It's not just local government. State government also lost authority under NCLB, and now what you're seeing are state legislatures reacting to the loss of control over the schools."

Roger Pfeuffer, superintendent in the Tucson Unified School District, says the power shift squeezing school boards is not a surprise, given what is taking place across the country.

"We don't have a concept of local anymore. It's state. It's national. It's global," Pfeuffer says. "People are not as altruistic about their neighbors. They want vouchers. They want open enrollment. They want all of these educational shopping options. For school boards, it means they have to deal with the whole concept of not being a monopoly anymore. It's a sad commentary, but community does not seem to matter as much as it once did."

The Rise of National Advocacy

Propelling these debates are a growing number of well-funded national advocacy groups, such as First Class Education, which touts the 65 cent solution as a way to inject nearly $14 billion into classrooms nationwide. Like other organizations that have sprouted up since the choice movement began, First Class Education relies on a simple message ("Money is wasted in education"), a simpler solution ("You have the power to stop it"), and few details on how it will actually work.

Anne L. Bryant, executive director of the National School Boards Association, says advocacy groups such as First Class Education "are far removed from local school districts" and are not concerned with the challenges educators face. Instead, she says, the rhetoric these groups generate "distracts school board members and educators from their real work, which is focusing on student achievement."

An analysis by [business consultants] Standard & Poor's, released in late November [2005], supported Bryant's comments, concluding that "no minimum spending allocation is a 'silver bullet' solution for raising student achievement." The analysis ... found "no significant positive correlation between the percentage of funds that districts spend on instruction, and the percentage of students who score proficient or higher on state reading and math tests."

Kids' Education Is in Danger

"These state and nationwide initiatives really have nothing to do with educating students," Bryant says. "On the surface, the 65 percent formula appears to be harmless, but as school board members know, there are many things that make up a student's experience in school that go far beyond what happens in the classroom."

Failing to recognize such nuances, critics of the 65 cent solution say, could be disastrous for public education, especially if states use a strict formula in developing the model. Under Kansas's current definitions, elementary art and music would not be defined as classroom instruction under the 65 cent rule. Librarians, counselors, psychologists, peer coaches, and mentor teachers also would not qualify.

"It's about the way you define it," says Brooks, whose district spends about 59 cents of every dollar on classroom instruction. "My argument is that if we are spending taxpayer dollars wisely, getting good results, and are still under 65 percent, then why should the state pull some arbitrary figure out of the air?"

Periodical Bibliography

The following articles have been selected to supplement the diverse views presented in this chapter.

Peter Cohn	"Conservatives Flag Concerns over Farm Disaster Spending," *CongressDaily*, September 22, 2004.
Matthew Cooper and Massimo Calabresi	"It's Your Money. He Just Spends It," *Time*, February 21, 2005.
Jan Erk	"Comparative Federalism as a Growth Industry," *Publius*, Spring 2007.
Nick Gillespie	"How Bush Outspends LBJ," *Reason*, December 2005.
Moira Herbst	"How Uncle Sam Spends Your Tax Money," *Business Week Online*, 2007.
"How Not to Spend 2.8 Trillion Dollars"	*USA Today Magazine*, December 2006.
"Indecent Proposal"	*Nation*, February 28, 2005.
Mary Clare Jalonick	"Is It 'Freedom to Farm' Or 'You're on Your Own?,'" *CQ Weekly*, February 14, 2005.
Dale Krane and Heidi Koenig	"The State of American Federalism, 2004: Is Federalism Still a Core Value?," *Publius*, Winter 2005.
Forrest Laws	"Parties Battle Over Depth to Cut 2006 Farm Spending," *Southwest Farm Press*, May 19, 2005.
Carl Pope	"Phony Federalism," *Sierra*, September 2005.
"Pork Busters, And Keepers"	*National Review*, May 8, 2006.
"Vital Statistics"	*National Journal*, January 27, 2007.

CHAPTER 3

How Do Government Spending Policies Affect the Economy?

Chapter Preface

According to the U.S. Office of Management and Budget, total federal government expenditure in 2005 equaled 31.5 percent of gross domestic product (the annual national income from goods and services produced in the United States), and states spent another 4.5 percent, according to the Center for Budget and Policy Priorities. Government spending is part of overall economic activity; the national government and the states account for well over a third of all the goods and services purchased in the United States. For example, the federal government purchases the services of engineers that design hydroelectric dams and the materials to build those dams. State governments spend on salaries for teachers and buy everything from textbooks to soccer balls for schools. These government expenditures have an effect on the overall economy. Analysts disagree over exactly how strong the effect is and whether it is a good or bad thing. Two areas of disagreement are deficit spending and infrastructure spending (whether government can help the economy by borrowing money or financing large projects like highways). Another controversial area is tax expenditures—targeted tax breaks to promote government goals such as having a large percentage of the population own their own homes.

Deficit spending—governments borrowing money to finance their budgets—is particularly controversial when funds must be borrowed from abroad. While foreigners continue to believe the United States has a strong economy and stable legal system, they are likely to continue to invest their money in the country. If the American economy falters, however, foreign investors might withdraw funds rapidly, causing the value of the dollar to fall and provoking even more flight of investment from the United States. The effect could be an economic catastrophe, claim some analysts. Other economists downplay this possibility, noting the historical strength of the United States, economically and politically. Some analysts believe that deficits serve to limit spending because there is a limit to how much debt politicians are willing to take on. Whether deficit spending is seen as good or bad depends on the overall view of government. People who believe that government spending leads to a better society think high deficits may limit spending on important programs. Advocates of limited government believe that high deficits can play a role in a "starve the beast" strategy, which limits the size of government.

Infrastructure spending is another area of controversy. Again analysts generally in favor of big government call for more expenditure, whereas others are skeptical of the need for large public works projects. Proponents of such expenditure believe that in the long run, things like bridges, roads, and education facilities pay for themselves in increased economic growth. Critics often paint such projects as "make-work" programs, which result in facilities that are not fully used by the public.

Controversy over spending extends to the tax system. Governments need taxes to finance their work, but they are also able to affect private citizens' behavior by giving tax breaks for certain expenditures. For example, governments encourage charitable contributions by allowing taxpayers to deduct them from their income, meaning they have to pay lower taxes. Likewise, the interest on home mortgage loans is deductible, encouraging home ownership. Critics of such tax breaks believe they benefit primarily the wealthy—after all, the rich have more disposable income to give to charity or to buy expensive homes. Proponents of deductions, however, hold that giving such incentives via the tax system is the most efficient way to channel private funds toward socially desirable projects.

In the end, viewpoints on these issues often come down to an opinion on the larger issue of the place of government in our lives. People who prefer smaller government generally oppose spending and support policies that limit growth of the public sector. People with faith in government hold opposite views. The controversies over government deficits, infrastructure spending, and tax expenditures presented in this chapter reflect a more general clash over the proper role of government.

> *"Our priorities are our military and pro-*
> *tecting the homeland. But on other pro-*
> *grams, we've reduced the growth of the*
> *discretionary spending."*

The Current Budget Ensures Security and Economic Growth

George W. Bush

George W. Bush was the forty-third president of the United States. Elected in 2000, he took office in 2001 and was reelected to a second term in 2004. In this viewpoint, taken from remarks on his 2006 budget, President Bush stresses the need to maintain spending on the military and homeland security. He also believes that taxes must remain low in order to spur economic growth and asks that the president be given a "line-item veto" in order to cut individual spending items that Congress puts in the bud-get.

As you read, consider the following questions:

1. What is President Bush's main priority when it comes to government spending?

George W. Bush, "Remarks on the Office of Management and Budget Mid-Session Review," in George W. Bush Administration, July 11, 2006, pp. 1315–1319.

2. What was the result, according to President Bush, of cutting taxes?

3. What, in Bush's opinion, is the biggest challenge to the nation's economic health?

When I came to Washington [in 2001], taxes were too high and the economy was headed into a recession. Some said the answer was to centralize power in Washington and let the politicians make the decisions about what to do with the people's money. That was one point of view.

Tax Cuts Spur the Economy

We had a different point of view. I believe that the economy prospers when we trust the American people to make their own decisions about how to save, spend, and invest. So starting in 2001, my administration worked with the United States Congress, and we delivered the largest tax relief since [president] Ronald Reagan was in the White House [1981–1989]. We cut rates for everyone who pays income taxes. We reduced the marriage penalty; we doubled the child tax credit; and we cut the death tax. We cut the tax paid by most small businesses, because we understand that most new jobs are created by small businesses. And we encouraged economic expansion by cutting taxes on dividends and capital gains.

Together, these tax cuts left nearly $1.1 trillion in the hands of American workers and families and small-business owners, and they used this money to help fuel an economic resurgence that's now in its 18th straight quarter of growth. The tax cuts we passed work.

Last year [2005], our economy grew at 3.5 percent, and in the first quarter of this year, it grew at an annual rate of 5.6 percent. Over the past 3 years, our economy has grown by more than $1.3 trillion, an amount that is larger than the size of the entire Canadian or South Korean economy.

Since August 2003, the U.S. economy has added more than 5.4 million new jobs. Our unemployment rate is down to 4.6

percent. People are working. Behind these numbers, there are American workers who start each day with hope because they have a job to help them build a better life. Behind these numbers, there are more families with more money in the bank for college tuition or a downpayment on their homes. Behind these numbers are small-business owners who are hiring more workers, expanding their businesses, and realizing the great promise of our country.

Budgetary Priorities

Our job in Washington is to keep this expansion growing—going and to promote progrowth policies that let Americans keep more of their hard-earned paychecks and aid us in reducing our fiscal deficit.

In order to reduce the deficit, you got to set priorities. And in working with Congress, we've set clear priorities. And the number-one priority of this administration and this Congress is to make sure men and women who are defending the security of the United States and helping to spread peace through the spread of liberty get all the help they need from our government. We will always fund the troops in harm's way.

In an age when terrorists have attacked our country and want to hurt us again, we will do everything in our power to protect the American homeland. Those are the clear priorities of this administration, and the clear priorities of the United States Congress.

Fighting a war on terror and defending the homeland imposes great costs, and those costs have helped create budget deficits. Our responsibility is to win this war on terror and to keep the economy growing. And those are the kind of policies we have in place. Some in Washington say we had to choose between cutting taxes and cutting the deficit. You might remember those debates. You endured that rhetoric hour after hour on the floor of the Senate and the House. Today's numbers show that that was a false choice. The economic growth fueled by tax relief has helped send our tax revenues soaring. That's what's happened.

Economic Growth Reduces the Budget Deficit

When the economy grows, businesses grow; people earn more money; profits are higher; and they pay additional taxes on the new income. In 2005, tax revenues grew by $274 billion, or 14.5 percent; it's the largest increase in 24 years. Based on tax collections to date, the Treasury projects that tax revenues for this year will grow by $246 billion, or an 11 percent increase. The increase in tax revenues is much better than we had projected, and it's helping us cut the budget deficit.

One of the most important measures of our success in cutting the deficit is the size of the deficit in relation to the size of our economy. Think of it like a mortgage. When you take out a home loan, the most important measure is not how much you borrow; it is how much you borrow compared to how much you earn. If your income goes up, your mortgage takes up less of your family's budget. Same is true of our national economy. When the economy expands, our nation's income goes up and the burden of the deficit shrinks. And that's what's happening today. Thanks to economic growth and the rise in tax revenues, this year the deficit will shrink to 2.3 percent of GDP [gross domestic product]. That's about the same as the average over the past 40 years.

Here are some hard numbers: Our regional projection for this year's budget deficit was $423 billion. That was a projection. That's what we thought was going to happen. That's what we sent up to the Congress: "Here's what we think." Today's [July 11, 2006] report from OMB [the Office of Management and Budget] tells us that this year's deficit will actually come in at about $296 billion.

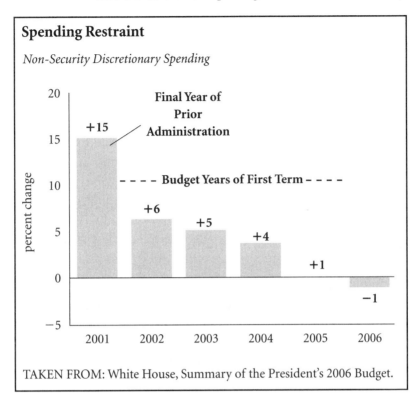

Spending Restraint

Non-Security Discretionary Spending

TAKEN FROM: White House, Summary of the President's 2006 Budget.

That's what happens when you implement progrowth economic policies. We faced difficult economic times. We cut the taxes on the American people because we strongly believe that the American people should lead us out of recession. Our small businesses flourished; people invested; tax revenue is up; and we're way ahead of cutting the deficit—Federal deficit in half by 2009.

Wasteful Spending Must Be Cut

As a matter of fact, we're a year ahead of fulfilling a pledge that I told the Congress and the American people. I said to the American people, give this plan a chance to work. We worked with Congress to implement this plan. I said, we can cut the Federal deficit in half by 2008—or 2009. We're now a full year ahead of schedule. Our policies are working, and I thank the Members of Congress for standing with us.

See, we cannot depend on just a growing economy, though, to keep cutting the deficit. That's just one part of the equation. We also got to cut out wasteful spending. See, it's okay to create revenue growth; that's good. But if we spend all that revenue growth on wasteful programs, it's not going to help us meet our objectives. And so the second half of the equation is for this administration to continue working with the Congress to be wise about how we spend the people's money.

Every year, Congress votes to fund the day-to-day spending of the Federal Government. That's called discretionary spending. In other words, the Congress decides how much to spend on these types of programs on an annual basis. Every year since I took office, we've reduced the growth of discretionary spending that's not related to the military or homeland security. I told you, our priorities are our military and protecting the homeland. But on other programs, we've reduced the growth of that discretionary spending. The last two budgets have actually cut this kind of spending.

The philosophy is clear: Every American family has to set priorities and live within its budget, and so does the Federal Government. And I thank the Members of Congress for making the tough votes, setting priorities, and doing the hard work on behalf of the taxpayers of this country.

We made good progress with the emergency spending bill that Congress approved in June [2006]. You might remember the debate leading up to that supplemental bill. And there was a good, constructive debate. And I weighed in. I said that we got to make sure that the emergency funding in the bill supported our troops and provided help to citizens that were hit by last year's hurricanes and to prepare for the dangers of an outbreak of pandemic flu. . . .

The Line-Item Veto

The next test is whether or not we can get a line-item veto out of the United States Senate. A line-item veto is an important tool for controlling spending. See, it will allow the President to target unnecessary spending that sometimes lawmakers put into large bills. Today, when a lawmaker loads up a good bill with wasteful spending, I don't have any choices. I either sign the bill with the bad spending or veto the whole bill that's got good spending in it. And I think it would be wise if we're seriously concerned about wasteful spending to enable the executive branch to interface effectively with the legislative branch to eliminate that kind of wasteful spending.

And so we've proposed a line-item veto that the House of Representatives passed. Under this proposal, the President can approve spending that's necessary, redline spending that's not, and send back the wasteful, unnecessary spending to the Congress for a prompt up-or-down vote. In other words, it's a collaborative effort between the two branches of government, all aimed at making sure we can earn the trust of the taxpayers. . . .

Dealing with Mandatory Spending

We're dealing with the short-term deficit, but there's another challenge that we face. In the long run, the biggest challenge to our nation's economic health is the unsustainable growth in spending for entitlement programs, mandatory programs such as Social Security, Medicare, and Medicaid. Millions of our fellow Americans rely on these programs for retirement and health care needs. They're important programs. But the spending for these programs is growing faster than inflation, faster than the economy, and faster than our ability to pay for them.

To solve the problem, we need to cut entitlement spending. We need to do something about it, is what we need to do. One reason Secretary [of the Treasury] [Henry] Paulson agreed to join this administration is because he wants to get something done about these entitlement programs, and I want to work with him.

You know it's so much—easy just to shove these problems down the road. The easy fix is to say, "Let somebody else deal with it." This administration is going to continue trying to work with Congress to deal with these issues. That's why I ran for office in the first place, to confront big problems and to solve them. That's why Henry Paulson made the tough decision to leave the comfort of private life to come in and do something good for this country. And the United States Congress needs to feel that same sense of obligation. The time of playing politics with Social Security and Medicare and Medicaid is over. We need to fix this for younger generations of Americans to come. . . .

Patience Needed

Let's just be patient about solving this Federal deficit; we're not going to take money out of your pocket; let's grow our way out of it. Let's keep—let's set priorities when it comes to spending and keep the people's taxes low, and these revenues will catch up into our Treasury. And they have. And we're reducing that Federal deficit, through the people's hard work and the wise policies in Washington, DC.

Today is a good day for the American taxpayer. Tax relief is working; the economy is growing; revenues are up; the deficit is down; and all across this great land, Americans are realizing their dreams and building better futures for their families.

> *"Low-income working families that need help paying for child care do not get it because of insufficient funding. Some of these families resort to inappropriate, unstable or unsafe child care arrangements."*

Critical Areas Demand More Government Spending

Robert Greenstein, Richard Kogan, and Matt Fiedler

In this viewpoint, a trio of authors from the left-leaning Center for Budget and Policy Priorities (CBPP) outline some critical areas in need of greater government spending. They believe that years of underinvestment have harmed the capacity of government to perform its job effectively. Although tough choices must be made, the authors believe the nation is willing to pay for programs that improve American competitiveness and enhance equality. Robert Greenstein is executive director, Richard Kogan is a senior fellow, and Matt Fiedler is a research assistant at the CBPP.

As you read, consider the following questions:

1. In what area has the chairman of the Federal Reserve called for more spending? Why?

Robert Greenstein, Richard Kogan, and Matt Fiedler, "How Should Policymakers Treat the Budget for Non-Defense 'Discretionary' Programs?" Center on Budget and Policy Priorities, March 13, 2007. Reproduced by permission.

2. What are the United Kingdom's goals regarding child poverty?

3. What is given in the article as an example of the need to improve the military health care system?

Various developments in the nation—and the world—are creating an imperative for increased resources for certain non-defense discretionary areas in the years ahead. These factors can be grouped into four broad categories: 1) meeting critical global challenges; 2) making American workers and businesses more competitive, and doing so in a way that helps to prevent income inequality from becoming still more severe; 3) addressing the challenges of poverty and demography; and 4) enabling government to perform its basic functions adequately.

Meeting Global Challenges

President Bush has spoken of the need for increased funding to fight diseases such as HIV/AIDS and malaria around the world, especially in very poor countries, and to help combat severe poverty and underdevelopment abroad through the Millennium Challenge Account [funds to help development in poorer countries]. From both a security and a humanitarian standpoint, these measures are important. Primarily because of overly tight levels placed on the appropriations committees, however, Congress has yet to fully fund the President's request in this area. (In 2007, the HIV/AIDS request is fully funded, but the Millennium Challenge Account is well below the President's request.)

The United States continues to rank near the bottom in the western world in terms of the share of its budget and its economy that it devotes to these matters. Increased resources are needed here and will continue to be needed for a considerable period of time.

The President and others also have spoken of the need for increased investment in alternative energy research. Climate change may be the single greatest danger facing the planet. Action to deal with it is needed on a number of fronts, one of which is energy research. This, too, will require more resources.

Improving U.S. Competitiveness

In an increasingly global economy, there is growing concern about jobs and economic activity shifting from the United States to other countries. There also is mounting concern over the rise in income inequality in the United States, including concern about how that trend could generate pressure to pursue polices that would make it harder to improve U.S. competitiveness in the global economy.

Among those who have recently voiced strong concern about growing inequality are President Bush, former Federal Reserve chair Alan Greenspan, and current Fed chair Ben Bernanke. Bernanke recently called for "policies that boost our national investment in education and training," noting that "a substantial body of research demonstrates that investments in education and training pay high rates of return both to individuals and to the society at large," as do early childhood programs.

Similarly, in recent testimony before the Joint Economic Committee, former Treasury Secretary Larry Summers called for boosting productivity by increasing investment in education, infrastructure, and research and development. He expressed concern at the "remarkable" decline in federal support for basic research and pointed to "key areas such as transportation and other infrastructure facilities where investment has been grossly inadequate." He also noted that "A growing body of evidence suggests that pre-school education has an enormous rate of return, particularly for children from a disadvantaged background, and funding for these kinds of programs should be a priority."

Addressing Challenges Related to Poverty and Demography

The United States tolerates a level of child poverty well above that of nearly all other western industrialized nations. For hard-headed economic reasons, as well as for humanitarian reasons and the good of the society at large, this matter ought to be addressed. (The United Kingdom has set a goal of cutting child poverty in half by 2010, and ultimately eliminating it, and has made impressive initial progress toward this goal.)

After years of experience with various programs, certain programs and types of interventions have been found to deliver results. Yet we underfund them. While a good part of the federal policy reforms needed to address poverty lie outside the discretionary part of the budget, some discretionary areas will need more funding if we are serious about making significant progress. They include Head Start, child care and early education initiatives, and housing vouchers, among others.

For example, millions of low-income working families that need help paying for child care do not get it because of insufficient funding. Some of these families resort to inappropriate, unstable, or unsafe child care arrangements; others have to forgo employment. Similarly, although studies have shown that families—and especially children—benefit when they use federal housing vouchers to relocate to lower-poverty areas with more jobs and better schools, only about one-quarter of the families eligible for vouchers receive any housing assistance due to funding limitations. Nearly 3 million low-income families with children now pay more than half of their income for housing.

Maintaining the Quality of Government Services

There are several areas where increased resources will be needed for the government to do an adequate job. One is IRS

[Internal Revenue Service] enforcement. The "tax gap"—the gap between what taxpayers owe and what is actually collected—is estimated at upwards of $300 billion a year. Expanded IRS tax enforcement is essential to reducing the tax gap; the IRS currently lacks the resources to do the job that is needed. Given the massive budget holes the nation will face in coming decades, this matter badly needs to be addressed.

There also is growing concern about the federal workforce. For years, the federal workforce has been squeezed down, even as Congress has placed more tasks on many federal agencies. A large cohort of dedicated, highly skilled individuals who joined federal service between the 1960s and the early 1980s is now approaching retirement.

Unfortunately, the workforce coming up behind these highly skilled individuals is, in many agencies, quite thin—in no small part because years of reductions in real resources for agency staffing made it difficult for many agencies to hire talented new blood in adequate numbers.

Tough Choices Necessary to Meet Critical Needs

There is growing risk that performance will decline significantly in the coming decade. While more is needed than simply infusions of resources, additional resources for staffing are a necessary (though not sufficient) condition to averting a marked deterioration in performance.

In certain other discretionary programs as well, multiple years of inadequate funding have had an adverse effect. One example is the national park system, which the Administration now acknowledges has suffered as a result of recent funding cuts; the Administration has proposed to boost funding for the parks in its 2008 budget, and additional increases may prove necessary. Another example is the military health care system, whose difficulties—exemplified by the problems recently uncovered at Walter Reed Medical Center—appear to reflect in part the lack of resources to handle the large number of servicemen and women returning from Iraq and Afghanistan. In cases like these, additional funds are likely to be needed to repair the damage caused by previous underinvestment. (The veterans' medical care system, which is administered separately from health care provided to active military personnel, as at Walter Reed, will need growing resources as well.) . . .

Savings can and should be found in various other discretionary programs to help pay for additional investments in the areas discussed above. The savings that can be achieved, however, are likely to fall well short of the costs of the needed investments. Addressing these issues will require an increase in overall funding for non-defense discretionary programs, which the nation should readily be able to afford if policymakers make the tough choices needed in other parts of the budget.

"Allowing government to grow beyond the public's willingness to pay for it in direct taxes is a sure path to endless government growth."

Concern Over Deficits Helps Limit Government Growth

W. James Antle III

W. James Antle III has written for many conservative publications and is currently associate editor of The American Spectator. *In the following viewpoint, Antle presents a brief history of the ideological struggle between "deficit hawks," who want to balance the federal budget, and "supply-siders," who are unconcerned about spending levels. Antle then makes the case that concern over the deficit is a necessary check on the growth of government, and that conservatives who see small government as an end in itself should be pushing to cut both taxes and spending.*

As you read, consider the following questions:

1. By how much did President Reagan cut taxes? Did the tax cut apply to all taxpayers?

W. James Antle III, "Confessions of a Supply-Side Deficit Hawk," *The American Partisan*, April 22, 2003. Copyright © 2003 W. James Antle III. Reproduced by permission of the author.

2. What action by Herbert Hoover does Antle claim made the Great Depression worse?

3. In the author's opinion, a truly fiscally responsible policy will keep which three things low?

There is a divide within the Republican Party on what constitutes the most important object of prudent fiscal policy: tax cuts or balanced budgets. We are seeing this division play out in the debate over President George W. Bush's economic stimulus package [of 2003]. The White House and the Republican congressional leadership believe it is crucial that we cut taxes to stimulate economic growth. Yet Sens. George Voinovich (R-OH) and Olympia Snowe (R-ME) provided the Democrats with the votes they needed to cut the latest Bush tax cut proposal in half based on their concern about the deficit.

A Long Ideological Struggle

Both sides of this debate can be said to have a storied ideological pedigree within the GOP [Grand Old Party, a nickname for the Republican Party]. Historically, Republicans have been viewed as the party of fiscal responsibility and sound money. They have resisted increases in federal expenditures on the grounds that the federal budget should be balanced annually and the national debt should be low. They applied the principles of personal financial prudence to macroeconomics and public finance.

This ultimately made the GOP the logical home of conservatives, who believed in smaller government for its own sake and the importance of abiding by constitutional strictures. Conservative opposition to deficit spending was an outgrowth of their opposition to growing the federal government beyond its constitutionally authorized size and cost. These conservatives similarly believed that it was important for producers to retain and enjoy the fruits of their labor, necessitating a low tax burden.

For Conservatives, Small Government Strengthens Society

Apparently we have lost sight of the conservative, as opposed to purely libertarian, reasons for limiting government. It is exactly because the welfare state cannot replicate the benefits of organic institutions like families, neighborhoods, and congregations; it can only make it easier for atomized individuals to live without these vital institutions. Welfarism tends to crowd out civil society just as surely as public spending crowds out private investment.

W. James Antle III, "Selfish Old Party,"
American Spectator, *December 21, 2006.*

Faced with the stagflation of the 1970s and the inability of Keynesian economic prescriptions to deal with it, a group of free-market conservative economists came to propound a theory known as supply-side economics. Whereas [British economist John Maynard] Keynes's theories were based on the idea that recessions were caused by insufficient demand that could be rectified by increased government spending, supply-siders held that the key to economic growth was stimulating the supply side of the economy through improved incentives. The best way for discretionary fiscal policy to influence these incentives was by lowering marginal tax rates, thus raising the opportunity cost of leisure while increasing the marginal value of labor.

Reagan-Era Tax Cuts

Congressman Jack Kemp (R-NY) and Sen. William Roth (R-Del.) became persuaded by this theory and offered the Kemp-Roth tax cut in 1978. Their bill would have cut marginal income tax rates by 30 percent across the board. Although the bill failed, it became the centerpiece of Ronald Reagan's economic agenda during the 1980 presidential campaign. After Reagan defeated President Jimmy Carter, he won the passage of an across-the-board 25 percent tax-rate cut. The result was an unprecedented economic boom that ended the years of stagflation.

But this was not the end of the story. Contrary to President Reagan's campaign promises, which reflected the traditional Republican advocacy of balanced budgets, persistent deficit spending and a doubling of the national debt followed. Many traditional Republicans joined the Democrats in blaming the tax cuts for the deficit and calling for a deficit-reduction strategy that included both new tax revenues and spending restraint. The Reaganites for their part countered that deficits were largely economically harmless and should be tolerated while supply-side tax cuts worked their magic (although the president himself remained at least conceptually committed to the idea that balanced budgets were desirable and rightly contended that pro-growth tax policies would lead to a greater tax yield in the long run). The deficit hawks and the supply-siders would find themselves in frequent conflict for many years thereafter.

Both Sides of Debate Wrong

It is here where we run into the worst excesses of both sides of this debate. Deficit hawks would like to imitate the failed economics of Herbert Hoover, who raised taxes in order to balance the budget during the Great Depression. These record income-tax rate and tariff increases further damaged the economy and actually prolonged the Depression, without helping public finances overall. More recently, George [Herbert Walker] Bush signed into law a deficit-reduction tax increase that worsened the 1990–91 recession, failed to cut the deficit, and played a major role in costing him his reelection in 1992. The budget-balancing effects of Bill Clinton's tax increase are wildly overstated. By raising taxes to balance the budget without regard for the counterproductive impact on economic growth, Republican deficit hawks are actually emulating the fiscal policies of such liberal Democrats as [former governors] Michael Dukakis [of Massachusetts], Mario Cuomo [of New York], Jim Florio [of New Jersey] and Gray Davis [of California].

Supply-siders for their part have become so nonchalant about the deficit that they tend to ignore government spending entirely. Jack Kemp used to decry aggressive attempts to cut spending as "root canal politics." [Financial columnist] Lawrence Kudlow has suggested that efforts to shrink government would be politically detrimental to cutting taxes. Some even go so far to say that the deficit is a positive good and that as long as tax cuts continue, growth in federal expenditures should not be particularly worried about. In this excuse making for big government, some supply-siders have in effect become little more than conservative Keynesians.

While deficits are often preferable to tax increases and their impact on interest rates in the context of the entire economy and world borrowing can be overstated, they are not a positive good. The Reagan boom would have been even greater without them. Just like taxes, government borrowing takes money out of the private economy and on balance should be minimized.

Concern Over Deficit Limits Government Growth

Allowing government to grow beyond the public's willingness to pay for it in direct taxes is a sure path to endless government growth. Concern for the deficit is a valuable check on federal spending. It must be remembered that high, economically self-defeating marginal tax rates stem from excessive spending. Cut the level of spending and progressively lower tax rates become sustainable. Even leaving aside their economic impact, it was the deficits of the 1980s that doomed supply-side economics and led to a partial reversal of the Reagan tax cuts. Deficit spending today will ultimately be the biggest threat to maintaining the Bush tax cuts.

Similarly, high taxes work against the deficit hawks' goals as well. Initially, they erode budgetary discipline and feed fiscally irresponsible public spending. Eventually, they depress economic growth which in turn actually reduces the growth of tax revenues. Balanced budgets are difficult, and usually not economically feasible, to achieve during slow or no economic growth.

The solution? Cut both taxes and spending. Shrink government to the point where it is only performing its constitutional functions and reduce taxes to accelerate economic growth. True fiscal responsibility involves keeping taxes, spending, and borrowing low.

Within Republican politics, the supply-siders and the deficit hawks need each other. But in terms of a rational fiscal policy, the American people need both of their good ideas, too.

> "We have become so dependent on additional inflows of very large amounts of foreign funds that any significant setback therein would have substantial consequences for our economy."

Financing Our Deficit Spending with Foreign Investment Is Risky

C. Fred Bergsten and Edwin M. Truman

In the following viewpoint, C. Fred Bergsten and Edwin M. Truman assess the impact that reliance on foreign investment could have on the U.S. economy. Foreigners hold over half of the Treasury securities that finance the government's deficit spending, and they are the major buyers of new debt. Although Bergsten and Truman don't think foreigners will liquidate (in other words, sell off) their U.S. securities, they are worried that they will stop buying new debt. The authors believe that the best way to prevent the harmful effects this could have on the U.S. economy is to run moderate surpluses in the federal budget, which will re-

C. Fred Bergsten and Edwin M. Truman, "Why Deficits Matter: The International Dimension," Testimony before the Budget Committee of the House of Representatives, January 23, 2007. Reproduced by permission of the authors.

duce the trade deficit and the need for foreign funds. Bergsten is the director of the Peterson Institute for International Economics; Truman is a senior fellow at the institute.

As you read, consider the following questions:

1. Between 1985 and 2005, how much of the *increased amount* of U.S. Treasury securities were purchased by foreigners?
2. According to the authors, what would happen if there was a substantial reduction in the inflow of new foreign investment into the United States?
3. What do Bergsten and Truman name as the "chief policy tool" that can be used to decrease the U.S. trade deficit, and thus reduce our reliance on foreign investment?

Foreigners account for about $2.2 trillion, or a little over half, of the outstanding total of $4.3 trillion of U.S. Treasury securities held by the public. Official institutions, mainly central banks, account for about 60 percent of this total. In addition, foreigners as a whole probably hold close to $1 trillion, or about 15 percent, of U.S. government agency securities.

These totals and ratios have risen rapidly over the past 20 years. From 1985 to 2005, foreigners acquired almost 75 percent of the overall increase in outstanding treasuries. From 1995 to 2005, domestic holdings actually fell while foreign holdings grew by twice the aggregate increase. Since 2001, foreign purchases of treasuries have accounted for most of the rise in the total outstanding.

These data raise the obvious question of whether the United States in general and the U.S. government in particular have become excessively dependent on foreigners to finance our domestic economy and indeed our federal budget. The ultimate concern is whether these holders, or perhaps some subset of them such as foreign governmental institutions, might precipitate a financial crisis by rapidly selling off large amounts of treasuries for economic or even political reasons.

Foreign Holdings of Treasuries

The answer to these questions is two-fold. First, we do *not* need to worry very much about foreign holdings of U.S. treasury securities per se. The U.S. capital markets are so large and so liquid, and the treasury market is a sufficiently modest component of it, that foreign shifts from treasuries to other dollar investments could readily be accommodated by a reallocation of the portfolios of other investors. We should worry even less about the risk of liquidation of treasuries by foreign official institutions, including the largest holders in Japan and China, who are the *least* likely sources of disruption of our financial markets in view of their responsibilities for financial stability and their institutional aversion to being blamed for any disruption of the world economy—and, unfortunately, due to the desire of many of these countries to maintain undervalued exchange rates to bolster even further their international competitiveness. . . .

When seen in this larger context of the entire U.S. capital market, foreign holdings are more on the order of 15 percent. This figure is considerably less than their share of 50 percent in the treasury market by itself. Foreigners hold only about 10 percent of U.S. equities and about 20 percent of corporate bonds.

This conclusion receives strong empirical support from the experience of the last few years. Foreign holdings of treasuries fell in 2000–2001, but the exchange rate of the dollar continued to rise throughout that period. Conversely, foreign holdings of treasuries rose sharply in 2003–04 while the dollar was declining steadily and substantially. There is simply no clear relationship between changes in foreign holdings of treasuries and the value of our currency.

Growing Budget and Trade Deficits Could Disrupt the U.S. Economy

There are obviously strong links between budget and trade deficits, and the deficit-debt dynamic relationships are very similar. At the same time, it is misleading simply to equate the two deficits, as is often done in the twin-deficit literature. Budget deficits typically involve a reduction in national saving and, if large, a steadily growing government debt-to-GDP [gross domestic product] ratio. They typically will not be corrected without explicit action. Trade deficits, on the other hand, typically involve an increase in foreign claims on the U.S. economy. As these claims grow in relation to national income, at least some natural forces are set in motion to correct the imbalance.

From a policy standpoint, neither deficit may be terribly harmful in the short run, and at least the recent fiscal deficits have been useful in stabilizing movements in output. Moreover, there is likely to be a credibility range in which debt levels could rise relative to GDP without much change in relative prices. In the long run, however, both deficits could become much more worrisome. There are forces tending to increase both deficits: political and demographic for budget deficits, income elasticities for trade deficits. At some point, continued large-scale trade deficits could trigger equilibrating, and possibly dislocating, changes in prices, interest rates, and exchange rates. Continued budget deficits will steadily detract from the growth of the U.S. capital stock and may also trigger dislocating changes.

Eduard M. Gramlich, Remarks Presented at
the Isenberg School of Management Seminar Series,
Amherst, Massachusetts, May 14, 2004. www.federalreserve.gov.

Total Foreign Capital Flows to the United States

Second, however, we *do* need to worry considerably about *total* foreign holdings of dollar assets and, in particular, the extent to which our economy has become dependent on new capital inflows to finance both our external and internal deficits because those inflows could slow abruptly or even totally dry up at virtually any time. Because of the direct impact of the federal budget position on total national saving, and thus on our current account imbalance with the rest of the world, I believe that this U.S. dependence on foreign funding is one of the major reasons we should adopt a national policy objective of restoring the modest federal budget surpluses that were in place as recently as 1998–2001.

At the margin, the role of foreigners in financing the U.S. economy is much more salient than suggested by the averages cited above: They accounted for virtually the entire increase in the total holdings of all U.S. long-term securities, including equities and corporate bonds, from 2000 to June 2005. It is true that this period is distorted by the sharp fall in equity prices after early 2000 and our ratio of dependence on foreign investors is considerably lower—though still close to 50 percent—if different base periods are chosen. But the United States has clearly become reliant on external funding for a very large proportion of the investment needed to fuel our domestic economy, and we need to carefully consider the implications thereof in setting national economic policy.

These financial flows are a manifestation of the very large and rapidly growing deficits in the U.S. merchandise trade and current account balances with the rest of the world. Those deficits hit $850 billion to $875 billion in 2006, about 7 percent of GDP [gross domestic product]. They have increased by an average of $100 billion annually over the past four years (and by an annual average of over $80 billion for the past nine years). Funding those deficits requires the United States to attract $3 billion to $4 billion of foreign money (including direct investment as well as financial capital) every working day. As a result, our net foreign debt had climbed to $2.7 billion at the end of 2005. In addition, the United States exports capital (including direct investment as well as portfolio capital) in the range of $500 billion to $1 trillion every year, which must also be offset by capital inflows.

Addicted to Foreign Investment

Hence we must attract $7 billion to $8 billion of foreign capital every working day to avoid significant changes in prices, mainly of interest rates and exchange rates but also of equities and housing, throughout the U.S. economy. Any substantial diminution of the total inflow of new foreign investment into the United States from this required total would have jarring effects on our financial markets and thus on our economy. The exchange rate of the dollar would fall, interest rates would rise, equity prices would almost certainly decline, and the weakening of the housing market would be exacerbated. The scale of these shocks would depend largely on whether the reduction in foreign inflows took place quickly, producing a "hard landing," or more gradually over a period of several years (as actually occurred in 2002–03 and again, albeit sporadically, in 2004 and 2006). . . .

Thus it would not require a *liquidation* of foreign holdings of treasuries, or any other class of dollar financial assets, to cause considerable problems for the U.S. economy. Such liquidations, from the current total of such holdings of more than $10 trillion, would obviously make the situation worse. But we have become so dependent on *additional* inflows of very large amounts of foreign funds that any significant setback therein would have substantial consequences for our economy. . . .

The Policy Response

The only effective response to this potentially severe threat to U.S. economic stability and prosperity is to substantially reduce the external deficit in our trade and current account balances. The goal should be to cut that deficit at least in half, to about 3 to 3[frac12] percent of GDP (at which level external funding might well be sustainable) rather than the 7 percent or so at present.

This will require a series of changes in economic policy in the United States and other major countries. One essential part of the package is to reduce the gap between saving and investment in the United States by a like amount of 3 to 4 percent of GDP, most or all of which should be accomplished by increasing national saving since reducing investment would weaken both our growth prospects and continued improvements in U.S. productivity. The chief policy tool that we can deploy with some confidence to promote achievement of this objective is a shift in the budget position of the federal government over the next several years from today's deficits of 2 to 3 percent of GDP to modest surpluses à la 1998–2001....

I believe there are strong reasons to convert the current, and especially prospective, U.S. budget deficits into modest surpluses without appealing to these international aspects of the issue. But the vulnerability of the U.S. economy to large and prolonged reductions in foreign capital inflows, especially if they occur abruptly, surely counsel that we "put our house in order" as promptly as possible. I am delighted that the committee is assessing these issues as part of its deliberations on the fiscal situation and hope they will help persuade you to adopt an aggressive stance to sharply improve the prospects over the coming budget cycle.

"The growth in tax breaks imposes costs on the economy and erodes confidence in the progressive income tax."

Tax Breaks Are an Inefficient and Inequitable Form of Government Expenditure

Eric Toder, Bernard Wasow, and Michael P. Ettlinger

The following viewpoint is taken from a report by the Century Foundation Working Group on Tax Expenditures. The group believes that the use of tax credits to encourage taxpayers to engage in certain sorts of activities—going to college, investing in certain products—is simply a form of government spending. However, unlike direct spending, tax expenditures (as the report calls them) allow politicians to appear to be cutting taxes when in fact they are often simply choosing an inefficient method of promoting a policy. The Century Foundation is a progressive research institute that promotes effective government, democracy, and free markets.

Eric Toder, Bernard Wasow, and Michael P. Ettlinger, *Bad Breaks All Around: The Report of the Century Foundation Working Group on Tax Expenditures*, New York: Century Foundation Press, 2002. Copyright © 2002 The Century Foundation, Inc. All rights reserved. Reproduced by permission.

As you read, consider the following questions:

1. About what percentage of the money required to fund federal programs is obtained from corporate and personal income taxes?

2. What are two benefits of limiting tax breaks?

3. Which income group might benefit from some tax breaks?

In 2001, for the first time in twenty years, Congress enacted major tax reductions. In addition to income tax rate cuts, elimination of the estate tax, and marriage penalty relief, Congress enacted new and expanded tax breaks amounting to about $275 billion over the next ten years. These included doubling the child credit and making more of it refundable, expanding tax benefits for pension plans and IRAs [individual retirement accounts], and expanding tax incentives for education, in particular, enactment of a new deduction for qualified higher education expenses. Congress did not, however, enact all the tax breaks that the president proposed in his budget, so we can expect some of these to show up in future legislation. Overall, the president proposed more than thirty new and expanded tax breaks costing $475 billion over the next decade. The tax bill did not embrace proposals such as a new refundable tax credit for health insurance, permanent extension of the research and experimentation (R&E) credit, extension of the deduction for charitable contributions to taxpayers who do not itemize deductions, and a new deduction for the purchase of long-term care insurance. The president also proposed new tax incentives for energy production and conservation as part of his energy plan.

Politicians Gain from Tax Expenditures

Why will such programs as health, education, child care, and energy production and conservation be paid for on the tax side of the budget rather than through direct expenditures? The answer is that special tax breaks allow the president and Congress to spend while appearing to be cutting taxes. The members of the Century Foundation Working Group on Tax Expenditures are concerned about this trend toward using the tax system to undertake disguised spending. It did not start with President [George W.] Bush: Democrats as well as Republicans are skilled practitioners. In the recent [2004] presidential campaign, for example, Vice President [Al] Gore proposed more than twenty new tax credits for various social and economic purposes. Such stealth spending makes for bad tax policy as well as inefficient spending. This report is meant to alert the American public to this practice and call for reform.

The federal individual and corporate income taxes currently supply about 60 percent of the revenues needed to fund federal programs. They are progressive in the sense that they take a larger share of the income of high-income than of low-income families. Indeed, income taxes are the main sources of progressivity in the nation's tax system; they offset the regressive effects of other large revenue sources such as payroll taxes (32 percent of federal receipts), federal excise taxes, and state and local sales taxes. Without income taxes, our ability to support adequate funding for national defense, public infrastructure, and a social safety net would be seriously compromised, and a much larger share of the tax burden would be shifted to low- and middle-income families.

Tax Credits Introduced by Congress

Yet the federal income tax and the agency that enforces it, the Internal Revenue Service [IRS], have become increasingly unpopular over the past few decades. The income tax, though still progressive, has become riddled with special benefits. Some of these benefits promote good causes, and some, such as the earned income tax credit, arguably belong in the tax code. But many tax benefits are difficult to justify, and the trend toward expanding them has accelerated in recent years. Since 1990, Congress has:

- introduced new tax credits for undergraduate tuition and lifetime learning and a new deduction for higher education expenses;

- expanded eligibility for participation in tax-preferred individual retirement accounts (IRAs), introduced a new, back-loaded IRA (the Roth IRA), and increased IRA contribution limits;

- introduced numerous new, special purpose saving incentives, such as medical savings accounts, education saving accounts, and preferential treatment of prepaid college tuition plans;

- introduced new, targeted incentives for investment and employment in economically disadvantaged areas;

- restored the tax preference for realized capital gains;

- greatly expanded the earned income tax credit, introduced a new child credit, and then increased it; and

- enacted many other tax incentives.

A Better Way

Regardless of the merit of any of the particular special benefits, the aggregate result is a highly complex system that imposes large compliance costs on taxpayers and makes enforcement more difficult, even as enforcement resources for the IRS are constrained. Special tax benefits increase resentment among those who do not qualify for them and endanger the voluntary compliance upon which the system depends. They also impose costs on the economy by diverting resources toward activities favored by the tax system at the expense of other activities that may be more productive. Of course, some

Tuition Credits and Pell Grants

In 1997 Congress enacted two major new tax incentives for postsecondary education—the HOPE scholarship credit and the lifetime learning credit. The HOPE scholarship credit helps students and families pay tuition costs for the first two years of undergraduate education. The lifetime learning credit is less generous than the HOPE scholarship credit but supports college education beyond the first two years, graduate education, and education and training later in life. These credits help middle-income families but, because they are not refundable, do not benefit families at the lowest income levels who most need assistance. Students from poor families, however, receive assistance from Pell Grants, a program on the spending side of the budget. An alternative to the tuition tax credits would have been to expand Pell Grants to provide more assistance to middle-income families. Use of the Pell Grant program for this new subsidy would have utilized an existing administrative mechanism and would have avoided many problems encountered in designing programs as tax incentives administered by the IRS. But expanding Pell Grants to the middle class would have made the nature of the subsidy more transparent, and that might have made it more difficult politically to enact.

Eric Toder, Bernard Wasow, and Michael P. Ettlinger,
Bad Breaks All Around: The Report of the Century
Foundation Working Group on Tax Expenditures.
New York: Century Foundation Press, 2002.

subsidies on the spending side of the budget also lack economic justification. But, inserting subsidies into the tax code can make them even more costly than they would otherwise be. . . .

We believe there is a better way. The key element in tax reform must be a thorough reexamination of existing tax breaks that would lead to elimination of many of them. Such reform is fully compatible with maintaining a progressive income tax as a major component of our revenue system while providing needed tax simplification. It is fully compatible with reducing the level of tax collections to return some of an anticipated budget surplus to the public, as in the recent tax bill. It also is compatible with maintaining or increasing collections to support existing or expanded funding of social programs, defense, or homeland security, or setting aside more resources to pay for the retirement of the baby boomers.

Limiting tax breaks will be difficult. But, spending less on tax expenditures makes it easier to keep rates low and to provide additional relief for low- and middle-income families. Restraining spending hidden through the tax code serves the goals of both those who want government programs to be more effective and those who favor a smaller and less intrusive government. . . .

Why Tax Expenditures Are a Concern

The Working Group recognizes that some tax breaks promote worthwhile objectives and does not propose indiscriminate elimination of all such incentives. But, we are deeply concerned about the growing tendency to funnel more and more social and economic policy through the tax code. The growth in tax breaks imposes costs on the economy and erodes confidence in the progressive income tax. It conceals the growth in government intervention in the economy by making new programs look like tax cuts. Moreover, in most cases, direct spending programs could accomplish more effectively the goals that tax incentives are meant to advance.

Tax breaks in many cases impose costs on the economy. They interfere with market incentives, channeling resources toward tax-favored activities at the expense of others with higher returns. They make the tax laws much more complex, requiring numerous fine distinctions between those activities or taxpayers that do or do not qualify for benefits. This complexity raises compliance costs for both individual and business taxpayers and makes it more difficult and costly for the IRS to administer the law. Even when taxpayers can reduce these problems by using tax software, the multiplicity of special provisions makes it much harder for them to understand how their tax liability is calculated.

Tax breaks allow some people to pay much less tax than others with the same income. This favorable treatment of some taxpayers fosters resentment not only among those who cannot use the breaks but also among some who object to the complexity even as they use tax incentives. Taxpayer frustration and resentment endanger the voluntary compliance upon which tax administration depends.

Many tax breaks serve important social and economic goals. The earned income tax credit lifts the income of many working families above the poverty line and eases the transition from welfare to work. Other incentives encourage employers to provide health care for their workers and to support charitable giving. Tax incentives account for a significant share of federal support for health care for the non-elderly, housing, and saving for retirement.

But often tax incentives are inferior substitutes for direct spending. The political climate encourages the use of the tax system to fund new programs because the public has accepted the notion that spending is "bad" and tax cuts are "good." New tax breaks allow politicians to have their cake and eat it too—providing new programs and special benefits for favored constituencies while appearing to support a smaller and less intrusive government. . . .

Why Not a Direct Expenditure?

For any proposed new tax expenditure, policymakers should consider whether its stated objectives might be achieved more effectively through a spending program. In contrast to tax breaks, spending programs are more transparent because their costs are made explicit and their overall contribution to public activity in the economy is apparent. This increased transparency facilitates democratic decisionmaking.

We emphasize that many proposed tax breaks would not receive serious consideration if the identical program design were presented as a spending initiative with payments made by a program agency instead of as tax rebates administered by the IRS. If a program cannot pass muster as new spending, then it should not be enacted as disguised spending through the tax code.

In many cases, direct spending is preferable to tax breaks for additional reasons:

- Some programs require expert review to allocate scarce budgetary resources (grants for scientific research or subsidies to promote the use of energy-efficient technologies). In those cases, it is best to use spending instead of tax credits. The IRS lacks the expertise and institutional culture to perform social services or program evaluations; its job is collecting and refunding taxes. If the IRS must be used, its role is best limited to distributing cash according to specific and readily quantifiable criteria.

- For some programs, the ideal time frame for eligibility assessment or frequency of payment may differ from the annual accounting period of the income tax. Recipients of benefit programs (food stamps, health insurance subsidies) typically need to receive cash benefits more often than annually. Other programs may base payments on a longer period of measurement (for example, Social Security benefits depend on the highest thirty-five years of earnings) and therefore do not fit the annual period for measuring income.

- Where Congress is especially concerned about abuse or fraud, more detailed monitoring by a program agency is preferable to random audits at the relatively low rate (much less than 1 percent) used by the IRS. A congressional directive to raise the audit rate applied to any specific tax break could improve the enforcement of that provision. But singling out one provision for more intensive scrutiny would divert resources from audits that produce more revenue and would lead to complaints about discriminatory enforcement of the tax law.

A Few Tax Credits Worthwhile

That being said, the Working Group recognizes that sometimes it is more cost-effective to use the tax system instead of a new spending program to make payments. Tax incentives avoid the need to create a new agency, although they do impose an additional burden on the IRS. A tax break can be a low-cost way to pay benefits when such benefits depend on objectively measured standards (such as the amount of home mortgage interest paid). And, using tax returns lowers costs if eligibility for assistance depends on data that are already reported to the IRS (such as income or number of dependents with Social Security numbers).

The tax system also may have some advantages as a way of delivering benefits that are limited to the working poor. This group, with incomes roughly in the $10,000–$30,000 range, has relatively few programs targeted to it, so there are few existing agencies that might handle the necessary administration on their behalf. Tax benefits also are more "user-friendly" than spending programs because beneficiaries can self-report eligibility on their return instead of applying to a special agency for benefits. Working people who may merit support based on economic need but do not wish to be stigmatized as "welfare recipients" are more likely to claim a tax benefit than participate in a spending program. The flip side of greater participation with a tax break, however, is that there also might be a higher rate of excess claims by those who do not qualify for the benefit.

Periodical Bibliography

The following articles have been selected to supplement the diverse views presented in this chapter.

Jill Barshay — "Tax Break: Mother of 'Innovation'?," *CQ Weekly*, April 4, 2005.

"Can U.S. Infrastructure Really Be Fixed?" — *USA Today Magazine*, January 2008.

Clive Crook — "'Starve the Beast' Doesn't Work," *National Journal*, August 11, 2007.

Nick Gillespie — "Goodbye to Big Government?" *Reason*, August 2006.

Government Accounting Office — "The Nation's Long-Term Fiscal Outlook," *GAO Reports* [GAO-08-783r], April 2008.

Ann Mettler — "Now What About Fiscal Sustainability?" *Business Week Online*, November 23, 2006.

"Mind the Tax Gap" — *Government Executive*, May 2007.

James Pethokoukis — "The Incredible Shrinking Deficit," *U.S. News & World Report*, February 19, 2007.

Jeff A. Schnepper — "Tax Shelters for You and Me," *USA Today Magazine*, September 2004.

Allan Sloan — "D.C.'s Deficit Math Doesn't Add Up," *Newsweek*, September 18, 2006.

Matthew Swibel — "Righteous Tax Credit," *Forbes*, November 29, 2004.

"Things Fall Apart" — *Nation*, August 27, 2007.

"United States Federal, State, and Local Spending" — www.usgovernmentspending.com.

CHAPTER 4

How Must Government Spending Change to Meet Future Challenges?

Chapter Preface

Government spending does not take place in isolation: money is spent to meet certain needs. Defense spending ensures the nation's safety, Social Security helps the elderly maintain a good quality of life, and infrastructure spending guarantees that we have good roads and schools. Over time the nation's needs change and government must change its outlays accordingly. Two of the major developments forcing changes in spending are the increase in the number of older Americans and the expansion of the War on Terror after the terrorist attacks of September 11, 2001.

The aging of American society is a chief concern of government budget planners. The youngest of the baby-boom generation will reach age sixty-five in 2010. They will then be eligible to receive full Social Security benefits. This development will be a burden on younger Americans—Generations X and Y—born during the "baby bust" because fewer actively employed workers will have to support a large retired population. Health care costs will also increase, as older people tend to have more medical ailments. No longer covered by employers' insurance programs, many older Americans will be reliant on government to pick up the tab for their visits to the doctor. Experts, such as the United States Comptroller David Walker, warn that significant changes must be made in financing health care and Social Security in order to meet these challenges.

The War on Terror has also caused changes in government spending. The 1990s saw a significant decline in military spending; the end of the Cold War meant that large conventional forces were no longer necessary to confront the Soviet Union. The World Trade Center and Pentagon attacks, however, spurred government to spend more money on defense. Considered part of the War on Terror, military operations in

Iraq and Afghanistan are costly. In addition, the pensions, disability payments, and medical costs for soldiers wounded in these conflicts will add to government spending for years to come. Homeland security spending will likely continue to increase as well. Terrorist groups are able to adapt rapidly to United States' defenses, requiring the constant development of new counterterrorist measures.

Aging and counterterrorism are hardly the only new spending challenges the United States will face. New interest groups will emerge, such as women's advocates and America's growing Latino population, to demand their share of the pie. Writers in this chapter present their views on what must be done if government spending is to adapt to future realities.

> "The demographic factor that is most important in terms of entitlement policy is the relative size of the retiree population versus the working-age population."

An Aging Society Will Require Reforms in Government Spending Policies

Dennis S. Ippolito

Because Americans are living longer and families are having fewer children, three major government entitlement programs will need to be reformed in the near future, according to political scientist Dennis S. Ippolito. Reforms such as means testing— paying benefits only to those whose income or savings fall below a certain threshold—may be necessary to preserve Social Security, Medicare, and Medicaid, the primary spending programs that benefit older Americans. Ippolito is a professor of political science at Southern Methodist University and author of several books on government spending and budget priorities.

Dennis S. Ippolito, *Why Budgets Matter: Budget Policy and American Politics*, University Park: Pennsylvania State University Press, 2003. Copyright © 2003 by The Pennsylvania State University. Reproduced by permission of The Pennsylvania State University Press.

As you read, consider the following questions:

1. What will the retirement age to receive Social Security benefits be in 2009? In 2027?

2. When does the Social Security Board of Trustees expect benefits paid out to exceed payroll taxes paid in to Social Security?

3. What is the "old-age dependency ratio"? Why is it important when discussing Social Security and Medicaid?

The post-2010 budget outlook is dominated by questions about three programs—Social Security, Medicare, and Medicaid. Spending for these programs now accounts for approximately 8 percent of GDP [gross domestic product], nearly double the level of just thirty years ago. If the current programs are left in place, costs are expected to rise moderately over the next decade but to grow much more rapidly thereafter. In 2040, for example, Social Security, Medicare, and Medicaid spending projections range from 15 to 20 percent of GDP. These long-term funding requirements have focused attention on entitlement reform. There is widespread concern that unless retirement and healthcare policies are changed, it may prove increasingly difficult to fund other essential federal programs and to avoid unacceptable levels of deficits and debt. What lends urgency to this concern is that any major changes in retirement or healthcare benefits would have to be made fairly soon, to allow future retirees ample time to adjust their financial planning. Proponents of entitlement reform, then, are looking to make immediate policy adjustments that will strengthen long-term budget control. . . .

Entitlement Growth: Long Term

To prepare for the new demographics of entitlement spending, Congress has scheduled future adjustments in Social Security retirement benefits. Under the 1983 Social Security Act Amendments, the normal retirement age for Social Security goes from sixty-five to sixty-six over a six-year period ending in 2009. A second increase, to sixty-seven, is scheduled for another six-year period ending in 2027. Early retirement at age sixty-two remains in place but at reduced benefits. At age sixty-two, retirees now receive 80 percent of full retirement benefits. This percentage falls to 75 percent by 2009 and to 70 percent by 2027, with the reductions phased in alongside increases in the normal retirement age. Eligibility for Medicare benefits, however, remains at age sixty-five. Despite these changes, the number of Social Security beneficiaries will grow very rapidly after 2010, and retirement costs will quickly escalate. In addition to the growing number of retirees, per-beneficiary costs are expected to climb because of longer life expectancy. Average life expectancy at age sixty-five is currently about sixteen years for males and twenty years for females. The Social Security Administration predicts that life expectancy will grow by an additional two years over the next several decades. These demographic changes will affect health-care costs as well as retirement benefits. Longer life expectancy, for example, is likely to raise healthcare spending even more rapidly than retirement costs.

Spending Composition

Under current policy, the budget shares and GDP ratios for Social Security, Medicare, and Medicaid would grow by sizable amounts over an extended period. Recent projections show the spending—GDP ratio for Social Security, Medicare, and Medicaid more than doubling between 2000 and 2040. By 2050, the GDP ratio could be even higher—more than 20 percent according to General Accounting Office (GAO) projections.

Funding requirements anywhere close to these levels leave little room for other programs without large tax increases or high deficits. The portion of the budget directed toward the elderly has been expanding for several decades, while the budget shares for discretionary programs and entitlements for the non-elderly have declined. If future spending budgets tilt even more heavily toward the elderly, the constraints on other programs would tighten still further. Moreover, current baselines exclude some emerging commitments likely to require substantial new spending—homeland security, environmental cleanup obligations, and contingent liabilities for federal insurance programs—so that the lack of flexibility in heavily encumbered budgets presents additional problems.

The composition of spending policy serves as a reasonable approximation of federal priorities. In the recent past, social welfare has emerged as the dominant priority, and, within the social welfare category, programs for the elderly have enjoyed the broadest political support and the strongest commitment in terms of funding. The needs of the elderly, however, inevitably have to be balanced against other federal responsibilities. As the GAO has warned, "Absent changes in the structure of Social Security and Medicare, some time during the 2040s government would do nothing but mail checks to the elderly and their healthcare providers. Accordingly, substantive reform of Social Security and health programs remains critical to recapturing our future fiscal flexibility."

Deficits and Debt

Another uncertainty about the long-term budget outlook is fiscal sustainability—spending commitments can be maintained without triggering unacceptable deficit and debt increases. The starting point here involves assumptions about future revenue levels. Long-term budget projections incorporate a revenue baseline of approximately 20 percent of GDP. This baseline represents current tax policy; it also reflects a widely held belief among policy analysts, however, that there is a ceiling on tax levels in terms of political feasibility. . . .

If political considerations and economic policy needs impose a comparable ceiling on future revenue levels, maintaining current spending commitments would lead to sharp increases in deficits and debt. When these increases actually begin to emerge depends on further assumptions, particularly those about the size and disposition of short-term budget surpluses. If the large surpluses originally projected for the next decade had been entirely devoted to reducing the publicly-held debt—the "save total surpluses" scenario—lower interest costs and related savings would have offset increased spending for a time, postponing serious problems with deficit and debt levels until after 2050. Saving only the off-budget surpluses would still have kept deficit-debt levels under control for several decades. Now, with on-budget deficits for at least the next few years, off-budget surplus savings are evaporating, and potential deficit and debt problems are drawing closer.

Gap Between Revenues and Spending

Regardless of short-term reductions in the publicly held debt, the projected growth of retirement and healthcare benefits would eventually threaten sharp increases in debt levels. In addition, the large trust fund balances that Social Security is expected to accumulate over the next ten to fifteen years are misleading in terms of the potential gap between revenues and spending. When Social Security benefits begin to exceed payroll tax receipts, which the Social Security Board of Trustees expects will occur around 2016, the difference must be funded through higher taxes, reductions in other spending, or borrowing. Trust fund surpluses make Social Security's claim on budgetary resources stronger, since the government owes interest and principal payments on securities held by the trust funds, but the actual funds to satisfy these claims must still be provided. The same conditions apply to the Medicare trust fund. Like Social Security, the Medicare trust fund is expected to have a negative balance between payroll tax revenues and benefit payments beginning around 2016. Since the Medicare trust fund surplus is smaller and the projected imbalance between revenues and spending greater, its projected insolvency is forecast for 2029, compared with 2038 for Social Security. The technical solvency of the Social Security and Medicare trust funds, however, is not the real issue. More important are the levels of taxation and spending required to support these programs. It would be possible, for example, to maintain the benefit obligations for Social Security and Medicare indefinitely by raising payroll taxes accordingly. The size of these tax increases, however, could be unacceptably high.

Dependency Ratios

The demographic factor that is most important in terms of entitlement policy is the relative size of the retiree population versus the working-age population. The old-age dependency ratio is widely used to illustrate the fiscal implications of population aging by comparing the number of potential workers (usually the population aged sixteen to sixty-four) to the number of retirees (the population aged sixty-five and over). With large numbers of workers per retiree—more than 5 to 1 in the United States in 1960—there is an ample economic and tax base to support the elderly. As this ratio drops, the economic and tax base shrinks, making it more difficult to fund expensive and fast-growing social welfare programs.

Through 2010, the proportion of the population aged sixty-five and over remains stable; between 2010 and 2030, the proportion grows by more than 50 percent. By 2030, more than 20 percent of the population will be over sixty-five, and about one-fourth of this group will be over eighty. The retirement of the baby-boom generation produces many more retirees, and longer life expectancy adds to the retirement and healthcare costs for these retirees.

Because of declining fertility rates, however, the working-age population to support these retirees is growing at a much slower rate than the elderly population. Fertility rates after World War II were well above 3.0 for nearly two decades but then began to drop. By the mid-1970s, the rate had fallen to less than 1.75; current rates are around 2.0 and expected to remain at or slightly below this level over the next twenty years. The effect of these contrasting demographic trends is a falloff in the number of workers per beneficiary. By 2030, the ratio of persons aged sixty-five and over to the working-age population is expected to be above 35 percent. The ratio to actual workers would be about 40 percent, which means a worker-to-beneficiary ratio of 2.5 to 1. In 2060, the projected ratio is even lower—approximately 2 to 1.

The fiscal problems associated with population aging are not confined to the United States. Most industrialized democracies are facing dependency ratios considerably worse than those of the United States; these ratios will necessitate proportionally greater retrenchments in social welfare commitments to the elderly. Indeed, a number of countries have already begun to implement reforms designed to reduce future obligations in their public pension systems. The common themes in these reform efforts are demographic adjustments and structural changes in social welfare systems.

Policy and Budgetary Reforms

The most straightforward demographic adjustment to population aging is to encourage people to work longer. The options here include penalizing early retirement, raising the normal retirement age, and providing extended transitions to full retirement through partial government benefits that supplement part-time work. In the United States, some of these adjustments have already been made. Benefits for early retirement have been scaled back, the normal retirement age has been increased, and the benefit penalty for work after retirement has been eliminated. In 2000, the Social Security "earnings test," which reduced Social Security benefits for high-income retirees who continued to work from ages sixty-five to sixty-nine, was repealed.

A second category of reforms directly targets program costs by reducing benefits through lower income replacement rates (that is, the relationship between pre- and postretirement income), lengthier contribution periods for maximum benefits, and stricter means-testing, or income eligibility, for benefits. Here again, the United States has already implemented benefit reductions for retirees by taxing Social Security benefits for individuals and couples with high postretirement incomes. Replacement rate formulas have been lowered for most categories of workers who will retire over the next several decades. Proposals for means-testing healthcare benefits have been discussed as well, but thus far there has been extremely strong opposition to means-testing benefits under Medicare Part A or premiums for medical insurance under Medicare Part B. When catastrophic health insurance coverage was added to Medicare in 1988, premiums were based on retirees' incomes, but intense reaction against this "surtax" led to the program's repeal the following year. It is possible that the addition of prescription drug benefits to Medicare would incorporate a means-test formula, but similar provisions for current Medicare program benefits appear unlikely.

> *"Those who believe we can solve this problem solely by cutting spending or solely raising taxes are not being realistic."*

Real Changes in Entitlement Spending Are Necessary to Prevent Fiscal Troubles

David M. Walker

In his capacity as comptroller general of the United States, David M. Walker heads the Government Accountability Office (GAO) and is responsible for presenting elected officials with information regarding the fiscal situation of the United States. This viewpoint, drawn from his testimony before the House Committee on the Budget, shows Walker's concern with the long-term financial situation of the federal government due to demographic changes that will affect entitlement programs—spending such as Social Security benefits that the government must pay to nearly all citizens.

David M. Walker, "Deficits Matter: Saving Our Future Requires Tough Choices Today," Testimony Before the Committee on the Budget, U.S. House of Representatives, January 23, 2007, pp. 13–18.

As you read, consider the following questions:

1. Why does Walker believe it is impossible to "grow our way out" of the projected budget deficits?

2. According to the author, if no major changes are made, by how much will federal spending have to be cut to balance the budget in 2040?

3. In what year will Social Security go from having a surplus to having a deficit? What are the three ways mentioned to cover the shortfall?

Since at its heart the budget challenge is a debate about the allocation of limited resources, the budget process can and should play a key role in helping to address our long-term fiscal challenge and the broader challenge of modernizing government for the 21st century. I have said that Washington suffers from myopia and tunnel vision. This can be especially true in the budget debate in which we focus on one program at a time and the deficit for a single year or possibly the costs over 5 years without asking about the bigger picture and whether the long term is getting better or worse. We at GAO [Government Accountability Office] are in the transparency and accountability business. Therefore it should come as no surprise that I believe we need to increase the understanding of and focus on the long term in our policy and budget debates. To that end—as I noted earlier—I have been talking with a number of Members of the Senate and the House as well as various groups concerned about this issue concerning a number of steps that might help.

Critical Elements of Budget Reform

Let me highlight several critical elements here.

- The President's budget proposal should again cover 10 years. This is especially important given that some policies—both spending and tax—cost significantly more (or lose significantly more revenue) in the second 5 years than in the first. In addition, the budget should disclose the impact of major tax or spending proposals on the short, medium, and long term.

- The executive branch should also provide information on fiscal exposures—both spending programs and tax expenditures—that is, the long-term budget costs represented by current individual programs, policies, or activities as well as the total.

- The budget process needs to pay more attention to the long-term implication of the choices being debated. For example, elected representatives should be provided with more explicit information on the long-term costs of any major tax or spending proposal before it is voted upon. It is sobering to recall that during the debate over adding prescription drug coverage to Medicare, a great deal of attention was paid to whether the 10-year cost was over or under $400 billion. Not widely publicized—and certainly not surfaced in the debate—was that the present value of the long-term cost of this legislation was about $8 trillion!

Of course, when you are in a hole, the first thing to do is stop digging. I have urged reinstitution of the statutory controls—both meaningful caps on discretionary spending and pay-as-you-go (PAYGO) on both the tax and spending sides of the ledger—that expired in 2002. However given the severity of our current challenge, Congress should look beyond the return to PAYGO and discretionary caps. Mandatory spending cannot remain on autopilot—it will not be enough simply to prevent actions to worsen the outlook. We have suggested that Congress might wish to design "triggers" for mandatory programs—some measure that would prompt action when the spending path increased significantly. In addition, Congress may wish to look at rules to govern the use of "emergency supplementals." However, as everyone in this [the House Bud-

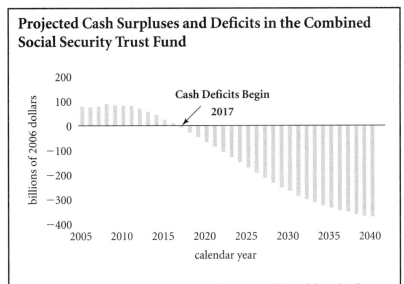

Projected Cash Surpluses and Deficits in the Combined Social Security Trust Fund

Cash Deficits Begin

2017

TAKEN FROM: GAO analysis of data from the Office of the Chief Actuary, Social Security Administration/David M. Walker, Testimony before the Committee on the Budget, U.S. House of Representatives, January 23, 2007.

get] committee knows, these steps alone will not solve the problem. That is why building in more consideration of the long-term impact of decisions is necessary.

No Easy Way Out

There is no easy way out of the challenge we face. Economic growth is essential, but we will not be able to simply grow our way out of the problem. The numbers speak loudly: Our projected fiscal gap is simply too great. To "grow our way out" of the current long-term fiscal gap would require sustained economic growth far beyond that experienced in U.S. economic history since World War II.

Similarly, those who believe we can solve this problem solely by cutting spending or solely raising taxes are not being realistic. While the appropriate level of revenues will be part of the debate about our fiscal future, making no changes to Social Security, Medicare, Medicaid, and other drivers of the long-term fiscal gap would require ever-increasing tax levels—something that seems both inappropriate and implausible. That is why I have said that substantive reform of Social Security and our major health programs remains critical to recapturing our future fiscal flexibility. I believe we must start now to reform these programs.

Although the long-term outlook is driven by Social Security and health care costs, this does not mean the rest of the budget can be exempt from scrutiny. Restructuring and constraint will be necessary beyond the major entitlement programs. This effort offers us the chance to bring our government and its programs in line with 21st century realities. Many tax expenditures act like entitlement programs, but with even less scrutiny. Other programs and activities were designed for a very different time.

Real Changes in Entitlement Programs Are Necessary

Taken together, entitlement reform and reexamination of other programs and activities could engender a national discussion about what Americans want from their government and how much they are willing to pay for those things.

Finally, given demographic and health care cost trends, the size of the spending cuts necessary to hold revenues at today's share of GDP [gross domestic product] seems implausible. It is not realistic to assume we can remain [with revenues] at 18.2 percent of GDP—we will need more revenues. Obviously we want to minimize the tax burden on the American people and we want to remain competitive with other industrial nations—but in the end the numbers have to add up.

As I noted, we need to start with real changes in existing entitlement programs to change the path of those programs. However, reform of the major entitlement programs alone will not be sufficient. Reprioritization and constraint will be necessary in other spending programs. Finally, we will need more revenues—hopefully through a reformed tax system.

The only way to get this done is through bipartisan cooperation and compromise—involving both the Congress and the White House.

Delay only makes matters worse. GAO's simulations show that if no action is taken, balancing the budget in 2040 could require actions as large as cutting total federal spending by 60 percent or raising federal taxes to two times today's level.

Changes Must Be Made Immediately

For many years those of us who talk about the need to put Social Security on a sustainable course and to reform Medicare have talked about the benefits of early action. Acting sooner rather than later can turn compound interest from an enemy to an ally. Acting sooner rather than later permits changes to be phased in more gradually and gives those affected time to adjust to the changes. Delay does not avoid action—it just makes the steps that have to be taken more dramatic and potentially harder.

Unfortunately, it is getting harder to talk about early action—the future is upon us.

Next year members of the baby boom generation start to leave the labor force. . . .

Reflecting this demographic shift, CBO [Congressional Budget Office] projects the average annual growth rate of real GDP will decline from 3.1 percent in 2008 to 2.6 percent in the period 2012–2016. This slowing of economic growth will come just as spending on Social Security, Medicare, and Medicaid will begin to accelerate—accounting for 56 percent of all federal spending by 2016 compared to 43 percent in 2006.

As I noted earlier, today Social Security's cash surplus helps offset the deficit in the rest of the budget, thus reducing the amount Treasury must borrow from the public and increasing budget flexibility—but this is about to change.

Looming Social Security Deficits

Growth in Social Security spending is expected to increase from an estimated 4.8 percent in 2008 to 6.5 percent in 2016. The result, . . . is that the Social Security surpluses begin a permanent decline in 2009. At that time the rest of the budget will begin to feel the squeeze since the ability of Social Security surpluses to offset deficits in the rest of the budget will begin to shrink. In 2017 Social Security will no longer run a cash surplus and will begin adding to the deficit. That year Social Security will need to redeem the special securities it holds in order to pay benefits. Treasury will honor those claim—the United States has never defaulted. But there is no free money. The funds to redeem those securities will have to come from higher taxes, lower spending on other programs, higher borrowing from the public, or a combination of all three.

I spoke before of how big the changes would have to be if we were to do nothing until 2040. Of course, we won't get to that point—something will force action before then. If we act now, we have more choices and will have more time to phase in related changes. . . .

Informed Americans Will Accept Real Changes

I have long believed that the American people can accept difficult decisions as long as they understand why such steps are necessary. They need to be given the facts about the fiscal outlook: what it is, what drives it, and what it will take to address it. As most of you know, I have been investing a good deal of time in the Fiscal Wake-Up Tour (FWUT) led by the Concord Coalition. Scholars from both the Brookings Institution and the Heritage Foundation join with me and Concord in laying out the facts and discussing the possible ways forward. In our experience, having these people, with quite different policy views on how to address our long-range imbalance, agree on the nature, scale, and importance of the issue—and on the need to sit down and work together—resonates with the audiences. . . .

The specific policy choices made to address this fiscal challenge are the purview of elected officials. The policy debate will reflect differing views of the role of government and differing priorities for our country. What the FWUT can do—and what I will continue to do—is lay out the facts, debunk various myths, and prepare the way for tough choices by elected officials. The American people know—or sense—that there is something wrong, that these deficits are a problem. If they understand that there truly is no magic bullet—if they understand that

- we cannot grow our way out of this problem;

- eliminating earmarks will not solve the problem;

- wiping out fraud, waste, and abuse will not solve the problem;

- ending the war or cutting way back on defense will not solve the problem;

- restraining discretionary spending will not solve the problem; and

- letting the recent tax cuts expire will not solve this problem;

then the American people can engage with you in a discussion about what government should do and how.

> *"The public investment deficit has received much less attention than the budget deficit, but it threatens our economic future all the same."*

Future Prosperity Depends on Government Investment in Infrastructure

Sherle R. Schwenninger

Sherle R. Schwenninger is director of the Economic Growth Program at the New America Foundation, a think-tank dedicated to exploring new ideas to meet twenty-first-century challenges. His viewpoint makes the case for establishing a federal capital budget. These funds would be devoted to improving America's highways, waterways, dams, and other physical infrastructure. They would also help improve information infrastructure, such as building more broadband communications networks. Finally the budget would support scientific research and education. Dedicating a special budget to these items would help indicate their importance for future economic growth and help preserve the funds from being used for other purposes.

Sherle R. Schwenninger, "A Capital Budget for Public Investment," *Ten Big Ideas for a New America*, Washington, DC: New America Foundation, February 1, 2007. Reproduced by permission.

As you read, consider the following questions:

1. Between 1950 and 1970 how much—as a percent of gross domestic product [GDP]—did the United States spend on infrastructure? How much since 1980?

2. What does Schwenninger see as the first step in repairing our "public investment deficit"?

3. What governmental entities currently use capital budgets? What are the advantages of distinguishing spending on infrastructure from other types of spending?

A strong and productive economy is the key to meeting our future fiscal challenges, from providing unmet entitlements to reversing our current account deficit. We need therefore to establish budgetary priorities that will make our economy more productive in the future. The government's current pattern of spending, however, does not reflect this imperative. Over the last several decades, the portion of the federal budget going to current consumption has increased, while that devoted to what might legitimately be called public investment has declined. Indeed, the federal budget does not even officially distinguish between spending on productivity-enhancing investment and spending on current consumption.

As a result, the federal government currently does not adequately fund investment in our nation's physical infrastructure or knowledge capital upon which a more productive economy rests.

America Is Falling Behind

From 1950 to 1970, we devoted 3 percent of GDP [gross domestic product] to spending on infrastructure—roads, bridges, waterways, electrical grids, and other essentials of a modern and competitive economy. Since 1980, we have been spending well less than 2 percent, resulting in a huge accumulated shortfall of needed investment. Not surprisingly, infrastructure bottlenecks—traffic-choked roads, clogged-up ports, uneven broadband access—are undermining our nation's efficiency. . . .

We are also now lagging behind in the infrastructure of the information age. Only 33 percent of households have access to broadband, which is increasingly critical for successful commerce. The United States now ranks 16th in the world in broadband penetration. And the costs of broadband in the United States are rising relative to those in other countries, putting American-based companies at a disadvantage. U.S. consumers, for example, are forced to pay nearly twice as much as their Japanese counterparts for connections that are 20 times slower.

We have also underinvested in basic science and research and development. Basic science research is important because it makes possible the technological breakthroughs that could revolutionize the economy and the way we live. It is also responsible for the innovation from which American companies derive premium returns on capital. But research and development spending as a share of GDP has declined over the last two decades, as the federal government's support for research and development has shrunk.

Finally, we have not kept up with other countries in the training of skilled workers, particularly scientists and engineers. The United States now graduates fewer engineers per capita than nearly all other advanced industrialized countries. Some American firms are thus beginning to complain about the shortage of skilled workers in some sectors of the economy, forcing them to rely more on outsourcing than they would like. In sum, underinvestment in research and development, a less than world-class infrastructure, and an inadequately trained workforce are acting as a drag on American economic growth and thus on future living standards.

How to Fix the Problem

Correcting this problem by ensuring that public investment is adequately funded in the future will require institutional reform. The United States underinvests in public capital in part because it neither properly accounts for its public capital expenditures nor properly finances them. The U.S. federal government is virtually the only government among the world's advanced industrialized countries not to have a formal capital budget that separates public investment outlays from current consumption expenditures. And unlike state and local governments, which use special purpose bonds to fund specific capital needs, the federal government finances public infrastructure projects out of general government revenues or out of special trust funds, like the Highway Trust Fund. This makes no sense since public investment is different from current government expenditures in both character and economic consequences. Most public investment, especially most public infrastructure projects, should be paid for over the useful life of the investment, and the fact that it earns a return on investment in the form of higher productivity and increased tax revenues should be reflected in how we account for it.

The first step, then, in correcting our public investment deficit would be to establish a formal capital budget. A federal capital budget would not alone correct the problem of chronic underinvestment in public capital. But it would make our government more accountable for its spending priorities and give us the tools to finance public investment in a way that is fiscally responsible. A federal capital budget would separate in a transparent way our nation's public investment from our government's current outlays. Capital budgets are used by private businesses—as well as by most cities and states—because they help management distinguish between ordinary operating expenses that a company routinely incurs during the course of doing business and extraordinary ones that add to a business's capacity to grow and thus should be depreciated over a number of years.

Discipline, Fiscal Responsibility, and Flexibility

Constructing a capital budget would help improve American government in three ways.

First, it would impose some necessary discipline on the discussion of our nation's budget and public debt. It is now too easy to become alarmed by growing deficits, on the one hand, or too complacent about shrinking deficits, on the other. Because the current budget makes no distinction between consumption and investment, it does not allow us to make intelligent choices about our spending priorities. The introduction of a capital budget would force a different and more productive debate over the budget. Above all, it would enable us more easily to ask the right questions: Spending for what purpose? Borrowing for what purpose? Without a capital budget, we are unable to differentiate good spending from profligate spending, virtuous debt from vicious debt. But with a capital budget, the public discourse would shift the discussion to a much more fruitful discussion of public spending for consumption versus public spending for investment. There will of course still be disagreements about the level of government spending, and the amount of public investment needed, but at least the debate will more likely address the right issues.

Second, it would allow us to develop a more sophisticated and more useful approach to fiscal responsibility. Today, the notion of fiscal responsibility tends to mean either a balanced budget or a balanced budget over a business cycle. Again, this overly simplistic idea fails to distinguish between the very different nature of capital expenditures and ordinary ones. With a capital budget, it would be easier to develop a consensus over some broad fiscal principles. In general, it would be reasonable to get centrists from both parties to agree that the current expense budget should be balanced over the economic cycle. And based on sound economic principles it would also be reasonable to be able to develop a consensus that a capital budget could be financed in part by government borrowing, which would be paid back over a period of years. Capital outlays would be seen for what they are—net additions to the government's capital stock, which like the capital assets of a company, would be depreciated over their useful life. Thus, with the initiation of a capital budget, additions to the national federal debt would be matched by additions to our national federal assets. Accordingly, the capital budget would provide a basic guideline for government borrowing. Any deficit that was incurred beyond the capital budget would need to be justified either as a matter of macroeconomic policy to stimulate the economy or as a matter of a national emergency. And over the years, the greater part of our national debt would gradually become the financial counterpart of our public productive capital, as the late eminent economist Robert Heilbroner suggested.

Third, it would also give us more flexibility for financing needed public investment in our nation's future while helping us maintain fiscal discipline over current expenditures. Today, we try to ensure a certain level of infrastructure spending by using trust funds with dedicated revenue streams, such as the highway and airport trust funds. But while this may ensure that these programs are insulated from budget-cutting pressures, it also ties the government's hands, reducing its ability to finance the optimal level and mix of public investment. Trust funds thus reduce the government's flexibility, and are subject to abuse by powerful political constituencies that can skew government spending. A capital budget would give the government much more flexibility to match government spending with our public investment needs while at the same time ensuring that public investment was adequately funded.

It would allow us to reduce federal spending on highways if that was warranted and increase spending on broadband without the current constraints imposed by designated trust funds. . . .

Conclusion

Overcoming the opposition to the establishment of a public capital budget will not be easy. But reintroducing the idea in itself would help spur a much needed debate about our nation's spending priorities and about the proper level of government debt. The public investment deficit has received much less attention than the budget deficit, but it threatens our economic future all the same. Properly accounting for what the federal government spends its money on and how it finances government expenditures goes to the very heart of sound modern government. For a nation that considers itself on the cutting edge of international commerce, it is an anomaly of historic proportion that we continue to deny ourselves this indispensable tool of modern capitalism.

> "Every woman's life is inextricably con-
> nected to what happens in Washington,
> no matter what her race, class, ethnic-
> ity, job, or family situation."

Government Spending Should Better Reflect Women's Priorities

Jane Midgley

This viewpoint presents the ideas of Jane Midgley, a public-policy analyst who has written extensively on the federal budget. Midgley notes that women occupy a special place in the economy, often doing work that is unpaid. They also have budget priorities that are different than men's, being more concerned with issues such as retirement security, education, and health care. However, because women are underrepresented among politicians, these issues are given less attention than areas such as homeland security and the military budget.

As you read, consider the following questions:

1. How much of the nation's economy, as a percentage, is made up by federal spending?

Jane Midgley, *Women and the U.S. Budget*, Gabriola Island, British Columbia: New Society Publishers, 2005. Copyright © 2005 by Jane Midgley. Reproduced by permission.

2. According to Midgley, what proportion of women are unpaid caregivers? How much is the estimated annual value of unpaid elder care?

3. What are five issues that women, on average, rank as more important than homeland security?

In the United States today we are surrounded by an abundance of economic resources that should ensure everyone has adequate food, healthcare, housing, education, and jobs at good wages. Instead we find ourselves falling far short of providing those basic needs for all our people. The economic resources we do have as a country represent the labor—paid and unpaid—of everyone in the United States. As workers, taxpayers, and nurturers within our families and communities, women are major contributors to this abundance. But do we understand the depth of our contribution? Are we in a position to tap into our current economic abundance for the good of our families, our communities, and ourselves? Can we envision a society in which everyone has access to that abundance?

Some Basic Definitions

Economic abundance includes three things: income, wealth, and assets. Income is financial gain that comes to a person in a given period of time from, for example, salary, self-employment or small business income, interest from investments, or gifts. Wealth is an accumulation of money that is held in bank accounts, stocks, and other financial instruments. Assets can include some of the elements of wealth, but assets are also things like land and buildings a person owns, other material possessions, and rights to future pension payments. In order to calculate the actual wealth and assets of a person, business, or country, liabilities (debts owed to others) have to be subtracted.

A budget is a forecast of what money will be accumulated and how it will be spent over a specific period of time. It is used to set priorities as well as to monitor what actually happens. For example, if you wanted to do a budget for your household for a month, you would include all the sources of income you expect for that month as well as all the things you need and want to buy.

The U.S. budget sets out the government's plan for the coming year, as well as recording the receipts and spending of previous years. The process of planning a budget includes making decisions on how to use other government resources beyond simply revenues and expenditures, just as your personal finances involve more than just your monthly income and expenses. The government's other resources include debt, savings, investments, and assets. . . .

American Women's Lives Linked with Washington, D.C.

The U.S. national budget is vast and has a powerful impact on communities across the United States and around the world. Federal government spending makes up a large portion of the nation's economy—almost 18 percent of the total goods and services produced—and the government exerts a strong influence on economic trends and the political and social well-being of the nation through taxation and spending policy.

Every woman's life is inextricably connected to what happens in Washington, no matter what her race, class, ethnicity, job, or family situation. From CEO [chief executive officer] subsidies to summer youth programs, food stamps to school lunches, Social Security checks to home mortgage deductions, a visit to the Grand Canyon to a drink of water from the tap, the budget decisions of the government affect women's lives on a daily basis. In spite of this, and in spite of the fact that women are full participants in the economy as workers and taxpayers and comprise over half of the population, they make up only 13 percent of the members of the U.S. Congress. This means our voices are not being fully heard, and our experiences and wisdom are mostly left out when important decisions are made. It also means that when the budget pie is being cut up, women and the families they support, alone or with a partner, can end up with the smallest slice.

In recent years, women, especially women of color, have been singled out and criticized for relying on national programs in the budget, and these criticisms have been used to justify cutbacks in welfare and housing subsidies. For instance, during the 1990s, advocates of reforming welfare argued that Aid to Families with Dependent Children (AFDC) was breaking the budget when it actually took just one percent of it. They promoted an image of welfare abusers—usually African American women, although only 40 percent of the recipients were African Americans—who received aid for many years. Most women on AFDC were women supporting one or two young children on their own and who needed transitional help to get back on their feet after a financial setback. The average time spent on welfare was only a few years.

Government Helps All of Society

In fact, all sectors of society depend on help from the government for housing (think home mortgage interest deduction), retirement money (Social Security), physical infrastructure (such as highways), healthcare (Medicare and Medicaid), and many other services provided by our national pooled resources. In addition, the unpaid and unrecognized work that women do in their homes and communities is the foundation for the productivity of the "official" economy and deeply affects national priorities as reflected in the budget. It is estimated that the value of unpaid elder care, for instance, is $257 billion annually, and that women are 6 out of 10 of the unpaid caregivers. If women did not provide this care, more public resources would need to be invested in paying for home health services, or longer hospital and institutional care. A Rice University study found that some caregivers lost substan-

Bush's Budget Hurts Women and Families

President [George W.] Bush's 2008 budget . . . continues on a troubling course. Under the President's budget, fewer low-income women and children would have access to health care, child care and early education, child support enforcement services, food assistance and other vital supports, and the education and training opportunities they need to get ahead. Social Security would be privatized, threatening the economic security not only of elderly Americans, but of millions of children. In contrast, the very wealthy would reap enormous benefits from the proposed extension of the 2001 and 2003 tax cuts and new tax cuts proposed in the budget. Less than a week after President Bush personally acknowledged growing income inequality, he has proposed a plan to make it worse, increasing the income and wealth of those at the very top while widening the holes in an already tattered safety net for the most vulnerable women and children.

National Women's Law Center,
"Increasing Inequality, Increasing Insecurity
for Women and Their Families,"
February 8, 2007, www.nwls.org.

tial work time and experienced a reduction of more than $10,000 in annual earnings. Women who cared for elderly parents were more likely to end up in poverty themselves than women who did not provide care.

Women have made strides in labor force participation and therefore in contributions to their families' financial well-being, and they make enormous unpaid contributions, yet they are not always rewarded by the economy. . . .

The Bigger Picture

The tragic events of September 11, 2001, and their aftermath changed the dynamics around the U.S. national budget, just as they changed so much else. The president's and Congress's response to the attacks on the World Trade Center and the Pentagon revealed that the United States has abundant national resources. Within days, the federal government made $40 billion available for disaster relief to New York City, emergency relief to victims' families, and increased security.

Where did that money come from? The fact that the resources could be made available so quickly illustrates that although the budget is a plan for how money will be raised and spent in a given time period, it is also flexible enough to respond to unexpected events and changed circumstances. This is a positive thing. It would be absurd if, in a budget of over $2 trillion, money could not be found to address the national needs after September 11.

It is a good idea to look deeper, however, if we are to understand the complex maneuvering that happens when so many resources are at stake. September 11 demanded a quick response from the government, but a quick response cannot take all relevant factors into account. A quick response also tends to favor those with ongoing access to decision makers. So, for example, an airline assistance act was passed a few weeks after September 11, giving $5 billion to the airlines immediately, and slated to cost $17 billion over five years. This act became law at a time when thousands of workers in the airline industry and other industries were being laid off, yet the aid was not tied to retaining workers or limiting CEO salaries and benefits.

Another example of the shortsightedness inherent in a quick national response is provided by the dilemmas faced by states in their budgeting after September 11. As the federal government rearranged the flow of money, it chose not to help states with their fiscal crises. Before September 11, states were already facing challenges. Because of the ongoing recession, they were receiving less income (unemployed workers can't pay taxes), and were dealing with more human needs (for instance many women who got off welfare to take a job were losing their jobs). September 11 also created a lot of new expenses as states and local communities had to beef up security. The national government faced all these things, too, but the difference was, as State Senator Sue Tucker of Massachusetts said, "States can't print money. We have to balance our budgets." Massachusetts—the state in which I live—faced a $1 billion deficit and began to slash programs such as higher education, homecare, substance abuse treatment, and instruction in English as a second language.

Military Versus Civilian Expenditures

When expenditures increase during an emergency, it is time to look at the tax side of a budget. There is an option to postpone or repeal tax cuts that have already been passed, or to increase taxes to cover the new expenses. However, the federal government and many states did the opposite in the last months of 2001. They continued to limit income to the system—by refusing to raise taxes—when the need for money to cover expenses was higher. The result was that those people with the least influence in the political process were more likely to see their programs cut so the budget could be balanced. . . .

Many members of the American armed forces and many Iraqis have been killed or injured in the war. In addition to the grief, pain, and stress this has brought to service people and their families and to so many Iraqis, the increased military expenses put a strain on the national budget and the resources available to address domestic needs. Typically, wars have had the effect of holding steady or reducing spending on social programs within the United States, and this is happening again. Over $150 billion has been spent on the war and the U.S. presence in Iraq so far, and additional expenditures—over $80 billion as of the end of 2004—are on the way. However, a CBS News/*New York Times* poll in January 2005 found that 57 percent of adults disapprove of the way President [George W.] Bush is handling the war in Iraq. If the war becomes increasingly unpopular, public opinion could challenge the scenario of continually escalating costs and casualties.

We can't use terrorism as an excuse for neglecting the human needs of our own people. The events of September 11 have understandably made everyone in the United States acutely aware of national security, and we do need to address legitimate security weaknesses that make people vulnerable to harm. Yet President George W. Bush's response to terrorism directed against the United States has eroded our civil liberties and increased economic and social pressure on immigrants and people of color in general. True national security comes from a strong democracy and internal well-being. Unless we have distributed our resources well and ensured that all families and children have adequate income, enough to eat, and decent housing, we are undermining what we want to protect.

Women's Perspectives

It is illuminating to look at women's perspectives on domestic priorities. In a survey conducted for the Business and Professional Women's Foundation by the Institute for Women's Policy Research in 2004, nearly nine out of ten women (86 percent) said that healthcare costs were of major importance, while just under half (49 percent) said homeland security was the most important issue. Homeland security ranked well behind retirement security (80 percent), job opportunities (71 percent), good schools (66 percent), and housing costs (61 percent) in a list of issues. Domestic security is important but not the most important thing, while issues of adequate healthcare coverage and retirement income are at the top of the list. These are issues that the national budget can more fully address on behalf of women and families.

> *"Although foreign aid is a central component of U.S. national security policy, spending on aid has lagged far behind the 'hard' dimensions of security since September 11, 2001."*

The War on Terror Requires a New Strategy in Defense Expenditures

Lael Brainard and Michael O'Hanlon

In the post-9/11 world, the United States needs a new strategy for spending defense dollars, argue Lael Brainard and Michael O'Hanlon, economic and political analysts at the center-left Brookings Institution. In the following viewpoint, they stress two areas where they believe the government is not spending enough to ensure our security: domestic security and foreign aid. Areas such as protecting critical private infrastructure and sharing intelligence information still need improvement at home. Abroad, the United States should spend more on combating poverty in order to win over the "hearts and minds" of Muslims and others in the developing world.

Lael Brainard and Michael O'Hanlon, "Reassessing National Security," in Alice M. Rivlin and Isabel Sawhill (Eds.), *Restoring Fiscal Sanity: How to Balance the Budget*, Washington, DC: Brookings Institution Press, 2004. Copyright © 2004 The Brookings Institution. Reproduced by permission.

As you read, consider the following questions:

1. How many more dollars per year do the authors believe are necessary to "fill the gaps" in homeland security?

2. What are the "six critical mission areas" of homeland security as defined by the Bush administration?

3. How much, in dollars, was the requested increase in the foreign affairs budget in 2004 compared with 2000? How much of a percentage increase was this? How does this compare with requested defense budget increases?

Since the attacks of September 11, 2001, much has been done to improve the safety of Americans, not only in the offensive war on terror abroad but in protecting the homeland as well. Americans, aware now of the harm terrorists can inflict, are on alert, providing a first, crucial line of defense. Air travel is much safer. Intelligence sharing, especially regarding individuals suspected of ties to terrorism, has improved. Suspicious ships entering U.S. waters are screened more frequently. Steps have been taken to reduce the country's exposure to biological attacks, and oversight has been tightened on labs working with biological materials. Private terrorism insurance is now backstopped by a new federal program. Well-known bridges, tunnels, and nuclear reactors are protected by police and National Guard forces when terrorism alerts so advise.

But much remains to be done. Most of the above steps respond to past tactics of al Qaeda rather than anticipating new ways that al Qaeda or other terrorist groups might try to harm Americans. Part of the answer is to continue to build the new Department of Homeland Security (DHS), especially those elements involved with border security, intelligence, and the federal government's interactions with state, local, and private efforts to improve the country's safety.

Filling the Gaps in Homeland Security

Far more urgent than creating a new bureaucracy, however, is filling the gaps that remain in the current homeland security effort. These range from creating a new networked intelligence capability to anticipate and prevent future terrorist actions, to better protecting private infrastructure like chemical plants and skyscrapers, to strengthening the Coast Guard and Customs (within DHS). They also include making sure first responders can communicate over commonly accessible radio networks during emergencies, hastening development of port security plans, and improving security of transportation networks aside from airports.

It is not possible to stop every type of terrorist violence. But by focusing on preventing catastrophic attacks, the United States can approach homeland security systematically and with a better chance of preventing future attacks on the scale of the 9/11 tragedy. That will take more attention from Congress and the administration—and more money, perhaps $10 billion a year (less than 3 percent of the defense budget) above what the administration proposed to spend a year ago, for a total of about $65 billion in 2014 in federal funding.

Homeland security is daunting in its complexity and in the sheer number of potential terrorist targets in an open country of nearly 300 million people.[1] As such, it requires a conceptual foundation and set of priorities. Recognizing as much, the Bush administration put forth a strategy for homeland security on July 16, 2002. Acknowledging that terrorists are themselves strategic, adaptive actors who will pursue new modes of attack and new weaponry, including weapons of mass destruction, the strategy emphasizes the crucial roles played by state and local governments as well as the private sector and individual citizens. Indeed, according to adminis-

1. As of 2004, the United States' population has surpassed the 300 million mark.

tration estimates, of about $100 billion a year in total national spending on homeland security today, the federal share is only about $40 billion.

More Spending on Domestic Protection Needed

The Bush administration approach involves six "critical mission areas": intelligence and warning, border and transportation security, domestic counterterrorism, protecting critical infrastructures and key assets, defending against catastrophic threats, and emergency preparedness and response. The administration also proposed four key methods, or "foundations," for enhancing all six areas: law, science and technology, information sharing and systems, and international cooperation. The administration's strategy makes a start, but it leaves out four key priorities for action. One is major infrastructure in the private sector, which the Bush administration largely ignores. A second is information technology and its proper uses, especially information sharing in government at all levels and between the public and private sectors. A third is the unrecognized need to expand greatly certain specific capacities for homeland security, such as the Coast Guard and Customs, as well as security for forms of transportation, such as trains. The fourth is intelligence reforms, especially the ability to monitor terrorists and to anticipate where their next attacks may come. Here the administration has fallen short. Incredibly, it has to date not even fully integrated the various suspected terrorist watch lists of various agencies.

Expanding these capacities in existing federal agencies will require more money, though far less than for the post–September 11 defense buildup. But annual funding for this federal responsibility, which has already doubled from roughly $20 billion to $40 billion, needs to grow further, to about $65 billion in 2014, if the country is to take reasonable precautions against future terrorist attacks that could be at least as destructive as those of 2001.

Build a National Homeland Security System

One of the highest priorities for federal spending over the long term must be investments that assist in creating a true national preparedness system—not merely supplementing the needs of state and local governments. Dollars that might be needed to equip every state and U.S. territory with sufficient resources to conduct each critical homeland security task could run into the hundreds of billions. Although the federal government has a responsibility to assist states and cities in providing for homeland security, it cannot service every one of their needs. Indeed, state and local governments are having difficulty absorbing and efficiently using the federal funds that are already available.

Federal funding should focus on programs that will make all Americans safer. That includes providing state and local governments with the capability to integrate their counterterrorism, preparedness, and response efforts into a national system and expanding their capacity to coordinate support, share resources, and exchange and exploit information. In addition, the federal government must enhance its own capacity to increase situational awareness of national homeland security activities and to shift resources where and when they are needed.

James Jay Curafano,
"Homeland Security Spending for the Long War,"
Heritage Lectures, *January 30, 2007.*

"Soft Power": The Foreign Affairs Budget

Even before September 11, 2001, many thoughtful observers worried that the United States was underinvesting in the non-military tools of foreign policy. Although funding has since increased substantially, we believe that there is still a compelling case for expansion relative to the CBO [Congressional Budget Office] baseline projection to effectively address infectious diseases such as HIV/AIDS and malaria, global poverty, complex emergencies, and America's new strategic interests. In many cases, such as the HIV/AIDS pandemic and the reconstruction of war-torn states, greater commitments of resources early on can diminish the overall cost to the U.S. taxpayer. And U.S. resources can also be leveraged by making the extra effort to build international support.

Over the past four decades, U.S. foreign assistance has been driven primarily by traditional national security priorities, especially the Cold War and developments in the Middle East. The end of the Cold War, disillusionment with aid's many failures, and the drive to balance the budget produced a slash-and-burn approach to the foreign affairs budget during the 1990s. Today American spending on foreign aid, never generous, looks paltry compared with that of many other wealthy nations. Although the United States is one of the top two donors in absolute terms (Japan is the other), it spends less relative to its income than any other wealthy nation. At 0.1 percent of GDP [gross domestic product], U.S. official development assistance is less than half the industrial country average of 0.22 percent. Per capita, U.S. aid of $35 a year is far below the industrial country average of $62.

Foreign Aid Spending Improves Security

Several recent developments argue strongly for increased spending on foreign aid. First, American resources are absolutely critical to combat the HIV/AIDS pandemic, a humanitarian tragedy of epic proportions that threatens to reverse impressive gains on child survival and health, life expectancy, productivity, and literacy in the world's poorest countries. Second, the acceleration of globalization has raised growing concern that unless the benefits are better shared, the divide between rich and poor could contribute to civil conflict, extremism, conflict over resources, and environmental degradation. Third, activists have developed a powerful recipe for mobilizing public support for greater international giving by focusing on a simple and compelling goal and enlisting high-profile public champions to help forge coalitions across the political spectrum. Finally, the post–September 11 War on Terrorism has greatly expanded the strategic calls on foreign aid—directly to reward allies, shore up frontline states, and rebuild Afghanistan and Iraq and indirectly to address the poverty that weakens states and provides space for terrorist networks to grow.

Although foreign aid is a central component of U.S. national security policy, spending on aid has lagged far behind the "hard" dimensions of security since September 11, 2001. For example, for fiscal year 2004, the administration requested an increase of $96 billion, or 31 percent, for defense; an increase of $24.4 billion, or 185 percent, for homeland security; and an increase of just $5 billion, or 22 percent, for foreign affairs, relative to fiscal 2000. . . .

Spending for Disease and Poverty Eradication

We believe that the new imperatives associated with combating killer diseases, global terrorism, and global poverty warrant higher growth in the foreign affairs account than elsewhere in the budget. But given how little the United States spends on foreign affairs and given projected declines in selected major components, our recommended increase is only about $11 billion above the baseline in 2014.

Although 40 percent of the foreign affairs budget—the development, trade, and investment and the politically allocated assistance categories—support economic activities, most of this is allocated among countries based on political considerations. Only about 10 percent of the foreign affairs budget is spent on development assistance in the strict sense that it is allocated according to primarily economic criteria. Development aid has recently received a boost from two directions. First, the growing consensus surrounding the urgency of the HIV/AIDS pandemic and our ability to effectively contain and combat it have expanded spending in this area. Second, the administration has proposed a large, permanent increase in bilateral development assistance of $5 billion a year by fiscal 2006, allocated through a new, more flexible and performance-oriented program, the Millennium Challenge Account (MCA).

Projecting to 2014, there are a variety of external estimates of the total price tag for combating global poverty and HIV/AIDS. The midrange of estimates of the cost of achieving the internationally agreed UN Millennium Development Goals for poverty reduction and human development (including fighting HIV/AIDS) implies a global increase of $65.6 billion over current expenditures by 2014. We recommend that the United States assume a share of this burden in proportion to its share of OECD income, which would imply a total U.S. contribution of $23.8 billion in 2014 (on top of existing programs in investment and trade), sufficient to fully fund the MCA and significantly increase funding for HIV/AIDS and growth and poverty reduction more broadly. While this increase would require significantly more resources in 2014 than the adjusted baseline assumptions, it is a sound investment that should yield dividends not only from a humanitarian perspective but also in boosting America's perceived legitimacy abroad and thus helping to advance our agenda internationally.

Winning Hearts and Minds

In many other categories of the foreign affairs budget, there is reason to expect spending to grow in line with or below the adjusted baseline projection. Both politically allocated economic assistance and security assistance for foreign military training and capabilities, which together account for more than 40 percent of foreign affairs spending, are slated to decline under agreements negotiated with Egypt and Israel, the largest recipients. Assistance to former Warsaw Pact countries can also be expected to decline. For humanitarian assistance, where public support is generally strong, the baseline scenario is compatible with growth in line with inflation and world population growth.

Since September 11, 2001, with growing concern that the United States is losing the battle of hearts and minds in the Islamic world, numerous task forces have called for substantial expansion of U.S. public diplomacy. Spending on diplomacy, which we define to include all State Department operational costs and public information activities, including broadcasting, has recently received a significant boost to upgrade embassy security, following declines in the 1990s. Although we support the calls for improved public diplomacy, even big expansions to these programs would have little impact on the overall budget, because of their relatively modest cost.

Overall, the foreign affairs account of the U.S. budget measures the priority America places on the exercise of diplomacy and foreign assistance. Over the next ten years, there is good reason to expect and indeed support continued real expansion in foreign affairs spending to combat threats to our national security from the HIV/AIDS crisis, global poverty, and global terrorism.

VIEWPOINT

"*We incur the costs of military forces and operations in order to reduce the losses from terrorist attacks or other external threats.*"

Spending on the War on Terror Is a Large Burden on American Households

Joshua S. Goldstein

Large numbers are easier to understand if broken down into figures we normally experience in our daily life. International relations professor Joshua S. Goldstein does just that; in this viewpoint he shows how much the War on Terror is costing individual households in the United States. He itemizes the total cost not just of military operations but also for items such as homeland security and the interest on money borrowed to pay for the war. He is careful to note, however, that these costs may be necessary to provide security from the greater costs of terror attacks.

As you read, consider the following questions:

1. How much are the costs of homeland security that are *not* included in the Defense Department budget? How much does this cost Americans per household per month?

2. According to the article, what is a conservative estimate of the total annual costs of borrowing money to pay for the War on Terror? How much is this per household per month?

3. Why does the author include costs of future terrorist attacks into the costs we all pay for the War on Terror?

The regular defense budget itself [in 2004], since a sharp post-9/11 [2001] increase, stands at $400 billion a year, or more than $300 a month per household. Of this, 95 percent is for the Department of Defense, with 5 percent for the nuclear weapons responsibilities of the Department of Energy. "The Pentagon," then, is the main claim on your household's contributions to the national defense.

Where the Money Goes

Pentagon expenses are themselves multilayered. Specific campaigns such as Iraq and Afghanistan—and potentially others—come and go side by side with an ongoing, worldwide effort to destroy Al Qaeda and other nonstate terrorist groups. All these and other military operations are overlaid on the routine maintenance of the world's preeminent military forces—costs like salaries, training, and weapons procurement. These "peacetime" costs are a necessary price of admission— our forces must be trained, weapons developed, and bases maintained—before military operations can occur. New types of spending in the post-9/11 wartime period add on more costs.

But the Pentagon is only two-thirds of the government's military-related spending. For one thing, the costs of homeland security outside the Defense Department add to the costs of wartime since 9/11. They come to more than $30 billion annually—$25 a month per household. Of that, more than two-thirds goes to the new Department of Homeland Security, with the rest spread throughout the federal government, especially the Departments of Health and Human Services, Justice, and Energy. Furthermore, various government agencies also perform national security functions that are not included in the Pentagon or Homeland Security Department budgets. For instance, the CIA plays a key role in the War on Terror and is not part of the Pentagon budget. And NASA provides infrastructure used extensively by military satellites. These agencies' contributions to national security cost on the order of $10 a month per household.

Costs of Benefits and Borrowing

The salaries of the soldiers fighting our wars are included in the Pentagon budget. But veterans' benefits are not. Those benefits supplement the fairly low salaries of soldiers and are an inducement for enlistment in the all-volunteer military. They are a cost of war, even though payment is delayed. So add them to the tab: $50 per month per household.

Now comes money we are paying out currently as interest on past military debts. We have sharply increased the national debt to fund military spending on various historical occasions, most recently during the [President Ronald] Reagan-era military buildup of the 1980s, in the last decade of the Cold War. We are doing it again, spectacularly, in the current war. It is hard to estimate how much of the accumulated debt is due to military spending. (Borrowed money goes into a big pot with other government funds and is spent for a range of government activities.) Anti-war organizations give various estimates, finding from one hundred billion to several hundred billion dollars a year in interest payments to be due to earlier military spending. To be conservative about this controversial item, let's put it at half of the low end of this range: $50 billion per year. That works out for the average household to $40 per month. It is a number that will increase dramatically in the next few years of ballooning federal deficits.

Finally, the war in Iraq was not included in the regular budget just discussed. Congress appropriated nearly $80 billion extra, mostly for Iraq-related operations, in the last half of the 2003 fiscal year, and $87 billion more for fiscal year 2004. (The government's fiscal year starts in October of the previous year.) In mid-2003, the Pentagon estimated that ongoing postwar operations in Iraq, narrowly defined, were costing $5 billion per month—nearly $50 per household. But with attacks on U.S. forces in Iraq increasing in late 2003, this number appeared likely to grow. The $87 billion supplemental appropriation for fiscal 2004, which included some non-Iraq expenses, came to nearly $70 per household per month. So we can take $60 per month per household as a pretty good approximation of the ongoing costs of U.S. activities in Iraq. Whether you think invading Iraq was a necessary part of the War on Terror or a mistake, we are there now and can't quickly cut these costs.

That's how your household's $500 monthly bill for government war-related spending adds up. . . .

Costs of Terrorist Attacks

A new kind of cost in this war is the damage to U.S. lives and property from terrorist attacks. The government will pay at least some of these costs. The damage to property and the economic losses from deaths and injuries in the 9/11 attack are hard to estimate in dollar terms. Most estimates range from tens of billions of dollars to more than $100 billion all told, depending on assumptions and methods.

The U.S. government has gotten into some trouble trying to estimate the value of lives lost on 9/11. It started with what seemed like a simple political idea, passed into law by Con-

The Monthly Bill For War-Related Spending Per Average Household

United States Government Washington, D.C.

The Smith Household

12345 Main St.

Anytown, USA

Amount due for war-related services rendered this month.

Your contract plan includes the following services:

Defense Department	$300 per month
Energy Department for nuclear weapons	15
Homeland Security	25
Other agencies	10
Veterans Affairs	50
Servicing past military debt	40
Iraq War	60
Total	**$500**

Note: Half of this total has been deducted from your paycheck this month. Currently your plan calls for borrowing most of the rest through the National Debt Credit Card Company. Please let us know if you wish to change plans in the future.

gress—that families of 9/11 victims would be compensated financially by the government. This would spread some of the burden of that trauma across all taxpayers instead of it being borne solely by bereaved families of those unlucky enough—or in some cases heroic enough—to have died in the attacks that day. . . .

The 9/11 victim compensation fund illustrates both the high economic costs incurred by the deaths of Americans and the rarity of anyone compensating those costs. Usually they are borne primarily by the survivors, the children, the companies where people had worked, and the communities where they lived. The deaths of Americans in the course of this war—at home and abroad, civilian and military—are economic costs, although of course much more than that. The economic costs generally are not counted, not charged to the government, and not included in what you pay for war at the parking meter in your living room. In the rare case, 9/11, in which government has tried to estimate and compensate for the economic losses, they turned out to be quite large indeed.

Future Attacks

An additional cost of this war—though impossible to measure ahead of time—is the damage that would be inflicted by future terrorist attacks on the United States. U.S. government policy is based on the assumption that future attacks probably will occur despite efforts being made to prevent them. Costs would depend on the type of attack. The effects of weapons of mass destruction would be far more expensive than, say, shooting down an airplane or bombing a resort. In the worst case, this war could see the destruction of one or more U.S. cities by nuclear bombs.

Insurance premiums reflect the best thinking by experts about the risks and costs of future events. Businesses facing possible losses from future terrorist attacks have turned to insurance companies for protection. But after 9/11, when direct losses were estimated around $40 billion, insurance companies withdrew coverage for terrorist attacks. The companies that provided any terrorism insurance in 2002 did so at very high premiums. This put potential target cities, especially New York, at a disadvantage in terms of businesses locating there, as Senator Charles Schumer explained: "Many in New York can't get terrorism insurance and those who can have been put at an extreme disadvantage because it's so expensive. This has basically hurt New York and other cities more than other places." In late 2002, Congress stepped in to guarantee insurance against terrorist attacks. The new law requires all commercial insurers to offer terrorism coverage and, after a few years of phase-in, to pay up to 15 percent of their premiums toward damages. The government will pay 90 percent of damages above $15 billion, up to $100 billion a year for the first three years. So the bottom line is that future terrorist attacks will ultimately be added to your bill for government war-related spending.

Negative Economics

The entire cost-benefit analysis of the War on Terror, and of war in general, rests on a negative kind of economics. The "benefits" consist of a reduction in losses. We incur the costs of military forces and operations in order to reduce the losses from terrorist attacks or other external threats. The situation resembles the choice you face if an armed robber demands your wallet. Giving up the wallet to save your life is clearly preferable. But if there is no check on armed robbers, eventually you will be accosted by them daily. So you will either buy weapons to defend yourself, or pay taxes to support a police force to protect you, or both. Either could be a worthwhile expenditure, if used well to prevent even higher costs, but they are still costs. And the same is true of a national defense budget. Losing a wallet or a city, paying for a gun or an army, training police or testing homeland security capabilities, all incur costs without generating wealth. There are exceptions, but this is the rule: war is an economic negative.

To recap, about $500 per month is what the government spends, per household, on war-related budgets, including veterans' benefits and homeland security expenses. About a third of this is the increase since 9/11. It will not bankrupt us, but it is a substantial cost.

Periodical Bibliography

The following articles have been selected to supplement the diverse views presented in this chapter.

David Baumann   "Priorities and Pragmatism," *National Journal*, February 10, 2007.

Ari Berman   "Looking Out for Veterans," *Nation*, April 2007.

Veronique de Rugy   "The Trillion-Dollar War," *Reason*, May 2008.

E. J. Dionne Jr.   "Time to Pay Up: There Is No Such Thing as a Free War," *Commonweal*, October 26, 2007.

Sandra I. Erwin   "How Astronomical War Budgets Threaten U.S. National Security," *National Defense*, November 2007.

John C. Goodman   "Government Spending on the Elderly: Social
and Matt Moore   Security and Medicare," *National Center for Policy Analysis*, November 2001. www.ncpa.org.

Thomas Kalil   "Planning for U.S. Science Policy in 2009," *Nature*, October 19, 2006.

"Keeping Promises   *AHA News*, January 22, 2007.
of Care"

Anna Mulrine   "The Third Battlefront: Money," *U.S. News & World Report*, October 30, 2006.

Shaun Pickford   "Social Security Problem Perplexes Candidates," www.politicallore.com, March 26, 2008.

David M. Walker   "Fiscal Stewardship: A Critical Challenge Facing Our Nation," *GAO Reports* [GAO-07-362SP], February 2, 2007.

George F. Will   "Many Strange 'Emergencies'," *Newsweek*, May 8, 2006.

For Further Discussion

Chapter 1

1. The authors of the first two articles—Shawn Macomber, and Nick Gillespie, and Veronique de Rugy—all share a view about whether large government expenditures are a good thing. What do you think this view is? How does this view contrast with that of Will Marshall and Robert Kuttner?

2. Dean Baker and Heather Boushey claim that more government involvement in health care funding will save money. What evidence do they present for this position? What are some potential drawbacks of more government spending in this area?

Chapter 2

1. How does Mark Zepezauer support his case that farm subsidies benefit mainly the rich? What examples does he give?

2. Chris Edwards focuses on overall levels of federal and state expenditures in order to promote the idea that more spending decisions should be left to the states. Ron Scherer focuses on health care spending, outlining some of the problems caused by spending decisions left to the states. How might the two authors' focus areas affect the reader? Do appeals to fairness have more impact when discussing health care than when overall spending is the subject?

Chapter 3

1. From his remarks, do you think that President George W. Bush has much faith in government spending to aid the

economy? What specific area of spending might be an exception to the President's general view of spending? How do the views of Robert Greenstein, Richard Kogan, and Matt Fiedler differ from President Bush's? What evidence do they use to make their case?

Chapter 4

1. Dennis Ippolito and David Walker both address changes in the age structure of the United States population in their viewpoints. Do they agree that an aging America is a problem? Are their solutions similar?

2. What device does Joshua Goldstein use to make it easy for the reader to relate to the amount of money spent on the War on Terror? Does his method work for you? What other methods might be used to make the large dollar amounts typical of federal programs comprehensible?

Organizations to Contact

The editors have compiled the following list of organizations concerned with the issues debated in this book. The descriptions are derived from materials provided by the organizations. All have publications or information available for interested readers. The list was compiled on the date of publication of the present volume; the information provided here may change. Be aware that many organizations take several weeks or longer to respond to inquiries, so allow as much time as possible.

Brookings Institution
1775 Massachusetts Avenue, NW, Washington, DC 20036
(202) 797-6000
Web site: www.brookings.edu

The Brookings Institution is one of America's oldest think tanks. Brookings's goal is to conduct high-quality, independent research to advance innovative, practical public-policy recommendations. The institution focuses on strengthening American democracy, advancing Americans' quality of life, and securing a successful international system. It publishes the *Brookings Bulletin* four times a year, as well as *Brookings Papers on Economic Activity*. Its major publications regarding government spending are titled *Restoring Fiscal Sanity*. These and many other policy papers are available at the group's Web site.

Center for Trade Policy Studies (CTPS)
1000 Massachusetts Avenue, Washington, DC 20001-5403
(202) 842-0200 • fax: (202) 842-3490
e-mail: jcoon@cato.org
Web site: www.freetrade.org

In association with the libertarian think tank the Cato Institute, the Center for Trade Policy Studies works to promote the benefits of the free market and limited government. The Center discourages U.S. protectionism, as well as trade barriers around the world, through trade policy debate. CTPS publishes briefing papers and policy analyses that are available on the Web site.

Center for Budget and Policy Priorities
820 First Street, NE, Suite 510, Washington, DC   20002
(202) 408-1080 • fax: (202) 408-1056
e-mail: center@cbpp.org
Web site: www.cbpp.org

This think tank sees itself as an advocate for working and poor people in Washington, D.C.'s debates over spending. Its Web site hosts policy papers on spending and budget policies in specific areas such as health care and Social Security. The center performs outreach, helping less affluent Americans obtain government benefits and take advantage of tax and spending programs.

Competitive Enterprise Institute
1001 Connecticut Avenue, NW, Suite 1250
Washington, DC   20036
(202) 331-1010 • fax: (202) 331-0640
e-mail: info@cei.org
Web site: www.cei.org

The Competitive Enterprise Institute focuses on proposing policies that would make U.S. businesses more competitive in the world market. Opinion articles, such as "Less Is More," and news releases, such as "Farm Bill Vote a Loss for Consumers and Taxpayers," show the institute's generally negative position on government spending. These and other items of interest are available on the group's Web site.

Economic Policy Institute
1333 H Street, NW, Suite 300, East Tower
Washington, DC   20005-4707
(202) 775-8810 • fax: (202) 775-0819

e-mail: research@epi.org
Web site: www.epi.org

The Economic Policy Institute's mission is to inform people and empower them to seek solutions that will ensure broadly shared prosperity and opportunity. It is particularly concerned with improving economic opportunity for working Americans. Papers and economic snapshots, such as "Economic Stimulus Essentials" and "Infrastructure Cuts and Consequences," generally take the position that government spending can help the overall economy.

Foundation for Economic Education
30 South Broadway, New York, NY   10533
(800) 960-4333 • fax: (914) 591-8910
e-mail: books@fee.org
Web site: www.fee.org

The Foundation for Economic Education is one of the oldest organizations dedicated to spreading the message of the free market to students and citizens. The foundation works to counter what it sees as antifree market beliefs, including antitrade beliefs. It publishes three periodicals: *The Freeman, Notes from FEE,* and *In Brief.* These publications frequently contain items critical of high levels of government spending, including "Does Government Spending Bring Prosperity?" and "Cutting the Budget" that exhibit the foundation's small-government philosophy.

Government Accountability Office (GAO)
441 G Street, NW, Washington, DC   20548
(202) 512-3000
e-mail: contact@gao.gov
Web site: www.gao.gov

The GAO investigates how the federal government spends taxpayer dollars. Headed by the comptroller general, a high-ranking federal official appointed for a 15-year term, the office works for Congress to investigate the efficiency and legality of spending. In addition, it projects spending needs and available revenues, warning of potential shortfalls in the federal budget. Its Web site posts reports on all types of federal spending. Such reports are available to the public, if they do not contain classified information, starting 30 days after their delivery to the requesting official.

Institute for Taxation and Economic Policy (ITEP)

1616 P Street, NW, Suite 200, Washington, DC   20036
(202) 299-1066 • fax: (202) 299-1065
e-mail: itep@itepnet.org
Web site: www.ctj.org/itep/

ITEP's mission is to keep policy makers and the public informed of the effects of current and proposed tax policies, as well as tax fairness, government budgets, and sound economic policy. ITEP examines state, local, and federal tax policy with an eye toward efficiency and fairness. Its publications regarding spending include "Tax Expenditures: Spending by Another Name," which examines how tax breaks are used to promote government objectives, and "Rainy Day Funds," which encourages state governments to set aside surpluses in case of economic downturn or other emergency.

Joint Center for Political and Economic Studies

1090 Vermont Avenue, NW, Suite 1100
Washington, DC   20005-4928
(202) 789-3500 • fax: (202) 789-6385
e-mail: general@jointcenter.org
Web site: www.jointcenter.org

In existence for three decades, the Joint Center for Political and Economic Studies is a research and public-policy institution whose work focuses exclusively on issues of particular concern to African Americans and other people of color. One of its main goals is improving the socioeconomic status of black Americans and other minorities. Part of this mission involves monitoring how federal, state, and local government spending affects these communities. Studies available on the

Web site include "Assessing the Cost of Mass Incarceration in America" and "Policy Implications of Children's Poverty"— both of which discuss issues that disproportionately affect black Americans.

The Office of Management and Budget (OMB)

725 17th Street, NW, Washington, DC   20503
(202) 395-3080 • fax: (202) 395-3888
e-mail: comments@whitehouse.gov
Web site: www.whitehouse.gov/omb

The Office of Management and Budget is an executive agency responsible for overseeing the preparation of the federal budget and ensuring that executive branch agencies carry out administration policies. The OMB devises and submits the president's annual budget proposal to Congress. Its Web site contains links to both the president's current annual budget and to historical data on the United States budget.

The Tax Policy Center

1775 Massachusetts Avenue, NW, Washington, DC   20036
(202) 797-6000
Web site: www.taxpolicycenter.org

The Tax Policy Center is a joint venture of the Urban Institute and the Brookings Institution. Nationally recognized experts in tax, budget, and social policy, who have served at the highest levels of government, author papers and reports concerning government fiscal policy, analyzing both spending and taxation. Examples of this work include "Facing the Music: The Fiscal Outlook at the End of the Bush Administration," a report critical of the 43rd president's policy on revenues and expenditure. It also issues shorter commentaries on new tax plans as well as spending programs. All of these publications and more can be found at the center's Web site.

Urban Institute
2100 M Street, NW, Washington, DC   20037
(202) 833-7200
Web site: www.urban.org

The Urban Institute researches issues that affect the well-being of the public, including housing, welfare, health, and education. Its work on spending issues includes *The Children's Budget Report* and *Kid's Share*, both of which focus on how young people are affected by government expenditures. The institute researches state and local budgets, focusing on how spending priorities at these levels affect children, the elderly, and the poor.

Bibliography of Books

Henry J. Aaron and Robert D. Reischauer
Setting National Priorities: Budget Choices for the Next Century. Washington, DC: Brookings Institution Press, 1997.

Greg Anrig
The Conservatives Have No Clothes: Why Right-Wing Ideas Keep Failing. Hoboken, NJ: John Wiley & Sons, 2007.

Arthur Benavie
Deficit Hysteria: A Common Sense Look at America's Rush to Balance the Budget. Westport, CT: Praeger, 1998.

James Bovard
The Bush Betrayal. New York: Palgrave Macmillan, 2004.

Lawrence G. Brewster and Genie N. L. Stowers
The Public Agenda: Issues in American Politics, 5th ed. Belmont, CA: Wadsworth/Thomson Learning, 2004.

Citizens Against Government Waste (Organization)
The Pig Book: How Government Wastes Your Money. New York: Thomas Dunne Books, 2005.

Timothy J. Conlan
From New Federalism to Devolution: Twenty-Five Years of Intergovernmental Reform. Washington, DC: Brookings Institution Press, 1998.

Alan Curtis
Patriotism, Democracy, and Common Sense: Restoring America's Promise at Home and Abroad. Washington, DC: Milton S. Eisenhower Foundation, 2004.

Chris Edwards and John Curtis Samples — *The Republican Revolution 10 Years Later: Smaller Government or Business as Usual?* Washington, DC: Cato Institute, 2005.

Robert Stowe England — *The Fiscal Challenge of an Aging Industrial World.* Washington, DC: Center for Strategic and International Studies, 2002.

Elizabeth Garrett, Elizabeth Graddy, and Howell E. Jackson — *Fiscal Challenges: An Interdisciplinary Approach to Budget Policy.* Cambridge, NY: Cambridge University Press, 2008.

John Steele Gordon — *Hamilton's Blessing: The Extraordinary Life and Times of Our National Debt.* New York: Walker and Company, 1997.

George Hager and Eric Pianin — *Mirage: Why Neither Democrats nor Republicans Can Balance the Budget, End the Deficit and Satisfy the Public.* New York: Times Books, 1997.

Stephen Holmes and Cass R. Sunstein — *The Cost of Rights: Why Liberty Depends on Taxes.* New York: W.W. Norton, 1999.

Julia Isaacs and Nelson A. Rockefeller Institute of Government — *Spending on Social Welfare Programs in Rich and Poor States: Key Findings.* Washington, DC: U.S. Dept. of Health and Human Services, 2004.

Bruce S. Jansson	*The Sixteen-Trillion-Dollar Mistake: How the U.S. Bungled Its National Priorities from the New Deal to the Present.* New York: Columbia University Press, 2001.
Robert E. Kelly	*The National Debt of the United States, 1941 to 2008,* 2nd ed. Jefferson, NC: McFarland & Co., 2008.
Grover Glenn Norquist	*Leave Us Alone: Getting the Government's Hands Off Our Money, Our Guns, Our Lives.* New York: W. Morrow, 2008.
Michael E. O'Hanlon	*Opportunity 08: Independent Ideas for America's Next President.* Washington, DC: Brookings Institution Press, 2007.
David Osborne and Peter Hutchinson	*The Price of Government: Getting the Results We Need in an Age of Permanent Fiscal Crisis.* New York: Basic Books, 2004.
Dimitri B. Papadimitriou	*Government Spending on the Elderly.* New York: Palgrave Macmillan, 2007.
Robert Patterson	*Reckless Disregard: How Liberal Democrats Undercut Our Military, Endanger Our Soldiers, and Jeopardize Our Security.* Lanham, MD: Regnery, 2004.

Peter G. Peterson	*Running on Empty: How the Democratic and Republican Parties Are Bankrupting Our Future and What Americans Can Do About It*. New York: Farrar, Straus and Giroux, 2004.
Irene Rubin	*Balancing the Federal Budget: Eating the Seed Corn or Trimming the Herds?* London: Chatham House, 2003.
Leonard Jay Santow and Mark E. Santow	*Social Security and the Middle-Class Squeeze: Fact and Fiction About America's Entitlement Programs*. Westport, CT: Praeger, 2005.
Daniel N. Shaviro	*Do Deficits Matter?* Chicago: University of Chicago Press, 1997.
Rob Simpson	*What We Could Have Done with the Money: 50 Ways to Spend the Trillion Dollars We've Spent on Iraq*. New York: Hyperion, 2008.
Gerald J. Swanson	*America the Broke: How the Reckless Spending of the White House and Congress Are Bankrupting Our Country and Destroying Our Children's Future*. New York: Currency Doubleday, 2004.
Michael Tanner	*Leviathan on the Right: How Big-Government Conservatism Brought Down the Republican Revolution*. Washington, DC: Cato Institute, 2007.

Bruce Wetterau   *Desk Reference on the Federal Budget.*
Washington, DC: Congressional
Quarterly, 1998.

Winslow T.   *The Wastrels of Defense: How Con-*
Wheeler   *gress Sabotages U.S. Security.* Annapo-
lis, MD: Naval Institute Press, 2004.

Len Wood   *Local Government Dollars & Sense:*
225 Financial Tips for Guarding the
Public Checkbook. Rancho Palos Ver-
des, CA: Training Shoppe, 1998.

Robert E. Wright   *One Nation Under Debt: Hamilton,*
Jefferson, and the History of What We
Owe. New York: McGraw-Hill, 2008.

Index

DeLay, Tom, 29, 32

Democracy, economics, 46–47

Demographic challenges, 110, 141, 145

Department of Education, 32, 79

Department of Homeland Security (DHS), 172, 182

Dependency ratios, 145–146

Direct expenditures, 133–134

Discretionary spending
  Bush, George, 31–32, 104
  caps, 150, 155
  education, 30
  elderly, 143
  farm subsidies, 30
  funding for, 110–112
  vs. mandatory, 29–30
  non-security, 103, 108

Disease eradication, 177–178

Divided government, 19

Dynamism *vs.* conservatism, 22–23

E

Economic issues
  abundance, 164
  Bush, George viewpoint, 99–106
  critical areas, 107–112
  democracy, 46–47
  dynamism *vs.* conservatism, 22–23
  globalization, 46, 176
  growth stimulants, 43–45, 114
  recession, 49–50
  See also Budget issues; Deficit concerns; Federal grant programs; Foreign investments; Gross domestic product; Spending issues; Tax issues

Education spending
  budget growth, 32
  community importance, 91
  control over, 87–89
  dangers, 92–93
  discretionary spending, 30
  federal grants, 74, 75
  national advocacy, 91–92
  NCLB, 77, 88, 91
  public investments, 44, 109
  state funding, 83, 90
  state level, 89–91
  student loan spending, 29
  targeted, 20
  tax deductions, 129
  tuition credits, 130

Edwards, Chris, 72–80

Egypt, 179

Elderly care, 143, 166, 167

Emergency spending bill, 104

Emerson, Jan, 85

Employer-based benefits, 51

Entitlement spending
  aging society, 141–142
  budget reform, 23, 141, 149–151
  changes, 152–155
  cuts, 38, 105
  demographic factors, 145
  growth rate, 25, 105
  long-term outlook, 151–152
  mandatory, 29–30, 32–33, 105–106
  See also Social security issues

Environmental concerns, 58, 63, 143, 177

Environmental Protection Agency (EPA), 14, 74

Ettlinger, Michael P., 126–135

peacetime defense, 182

pork-barrel spending, 24, 68, 70

questionable practices, 67–68

research and development, 158

women's priorities, 163–170

See also Budget issues; Congress/congressional spending; Corruption/waste in spending; Discretionary spending; Education spending; Entitlement spending; Fiscal spending; Medicare/ Medicaid spending; Politics of spending; Reform issues; Republican Party spending; War on terror

State Children's Health Insurance Program (SCHIP), 51–52

State government grants, 77

Stevens, Ted, 66

Student loan spending, 29

Summers, Larry, 109

Supply-side movement, 22–23, 117

T

Tax issues

anti-tax groups, 89

breaks, 100–101, 126–135, 131–132

credits, 128–129, 134–135

cuts, 50–51, 115–116

direct expenditures, 133–134

distribution of funds, 76–77, 127–128

mortgage interest, 97

reform, 26, 45–46, 131

social security, 147

tax gap, 111

See also Budget issues; War on terror

Taxpayers for Common Sense, 14

Terrorism. *See* War on terror

Title I education funds, 88

Toder, Eric, 126–135

Trade deficits, 49, 122

Treasury holdings, 102, 120, 121

Truman, Edwin M., 119–125

Tuition tax credits, 130

U

Unemployment rate, 100–101

U.S. Department of Agriculture (USDA), 61

Utt, Ronald D., 64–71

W

Walker, David M., 148–155

The Wall Street Journal, 42

Walter Reed Medical Center, 111–112

War in Iraq, 169–170, 183

War on terror

cost-benefit analysis, 186–187

cost of terrorism, 101, 183–186

distribution of funds, 181–182

foreign aid spending, 175–177

homeland security, 173–175

military spending, 169–170, 178–179

spending changes, 138

Wasow, Bernard, 126–135

Wasteful spending, 103–104

Weapons of mass destruction (WMD), 185

Wigglesworth, Ned, 83